TAP YOUR
A$$ETS

Also by David Demers

*ABCs of Buying Rental Property: How You Can Achieve Financial
    Freedom in Five Years* (ghostwritten for Ken McElroy)

*Jelly Beans & Peanuts: Life and Times of Llewellyn Jenkins,
    an American Banker, Soldier and Family Man*

*The Rest of the Story: Life and Times of
    Arizona State Senate President Leo F. Corbet Jr.*

*The Ivory Tower of Babel: Why the Social Sciences
    Are Failing to Live up to Their Promises*

The Luminar Papers: A Novel (a.k.a. *The Killing of Bere Baudin*)

History and Future of Mass Media: An Integrated Perspective

*How the Mass Media Really Work: An Introduction to
    Their Role as Institutions of Control and Change*
    (with Taehyun Kim and Daniel Erickson)

The Menace of the Corporate Newspaper: Fact or Fiction?

Global Media: Menace or Messiah?

TAP YOUR 🏠

A$$ETS

How to Achieve Financial Freedom in Two Years with JUST ONE RENTAL HOME

David Demers

MARQUETTE BOOKS LLC
PHOENIX, ARIZONA

LIBRARY OF CONGRESS CATALOGING-IN-PUBLICATION DATA

Names: Demers, David, 1953- author.

Title: Tap your a$$ets : how to achieve financial freedom in two years with just one rental home / David Demers.

Other titles: Tap your assets

Description: Phoenix, Arizona : Marquette Books LLC, [2024] | Includes bibliographical references and index. | Summary: "In 2020, real estate ghostwriter and retired professor David Demers was in a financial pickle. A recent divorce meant he was now paying all of the bills for himself and his daughter, who was in college. His Social Security check and ghostwriting income weren't enough to cover all expenses. So, at age 67, he tapped his assets (borrowed on the equity in his home), purchased a condo to live in, and began leasing his modest Phoenix home through Airbnb and Vrbo. A year later his financial problem was solved. His rental home was generating more than $43,000 in annual profits. In Tap Your Assets, Dr. Dave shows you how to purchase a house for as little as 3.5% down and convert that or your existing home into a short- or long-term rental that can generate $50,000 or more a year in profits. Tap Your Assets also will show you how to (1) accurately estimate profits before you make a decision to buy, (2) create a limited liability company to protect your assets, (3) post your property on Airbnb and Vrbo or Zillow, (4) maintain your property and keep 5-star ratings rolling in, and (5) calculate interest and depreciation savings, and do your taxes"-- Provided by publisher.

Identifiers: LCCN 2024005374 (print) | LCCN 2024005375 (ebook)
| ISBN 9798990005891 (library binding) | ISBN 9798990005884 (ebook)

Subjects: LCSH: Real estate investment--United States. | Real estate business--United States. | Rental housing--United States.

Classification: LCC HD255 .D448 2024 (print) | LCC HD255 (ebook)
| DDC 332.63/24--dc23/eng/20240308

LC record available at https://lccn.loc.gov/2024005374

LC ebook record available at https://lccn.loc.gov/2024005375

MARQUETTE BOOKS LLC, 16421 N 31st Ave, Phoenix, Arizona 85053
www.MarquetteBooks.com • MarquetteBooksLLC@gmail.com • 1-623-363-4668

What You Will Learn in this Book

1. Why rental real estate investing is the safest and fastest way to financial independence (next to inheritance) and up to 25 times more profitable than the stock market.

2. How to estimate the profitability of your proposed rental property before you purchase or convert it, and how to cover your assets should your short-term rental plan fail.

3. How to tap your assets and the assets of friends, family members, and others to fund your real estate venture.

4. How to set up a limited liability company (LLC), decorate your property, post your property on Airbnb and Vrbo, manage your property, keep those 5-star ratings rolling in, and calculate your expected federal tax bill.

5. How to legally pay little or no federal taxes on your rental property income.

6. How to leverage your rental property to buy another property, even if your income is too low, to qualify for a conventional loan.

7. How to pay little to no capital gains taxes when you sell (and you don't have to use a 1031 exchange).

To my lovely daughter,
who has filled my life with joy

Contents

A Note from Dr. Dave

I am not a real estate mogul, nor do I aspire to be one.

I purchased my first rental property when I was 65 (*if I can do it, you can, too*).

I'm a real estate investor with modest dreams — to maintain my financial independence in old age. This doesn't necessarily mean great wealth. *Financial freedom is a state of mind where you never worry about paying the next bill.*

The advice I give in this book can't make you wealthy overnight.[1] But you can achieve financial independence in as little as a year or two, and you can generate more than $1 million in profits in 10 to 20 years with just one modest rental property (faster with two or a higher-priced property).

Skeptical?

I hope so.

That's the *first sign* of a sage investor.

---

[1]But real estate is the fastest way to wealth next to inheritance. Half of all wealth in America is inherited. See Facundo Alvaredo, Bertrand Garbinti and Thomas Piketty, "On the Share of Inheritance in Aggregate Wealth: Europe and the USA, 1900–2010," *Economica*, 84, 239–260 (2017), retrieved 7/23/23, from <www.piketty.pse.ens.fr/files/AlvaredoGarbintiPiketty2017.pdf> and Sam Pizzigati, "The 'Self-Made' Myth: Our Hallucinating Rich," Inequality.org (September 23, 2012), retrieved 7/23/23, from <https://inequality.org/research/selfmade-myth-hallucinating-rich>.

The *second* is courage.

If you are the type of person who always plays it safe, you likely will not make a good investor. Risk is an element of all entrepreneurial ventures.

But investing in rental real estate is far less risky than the stock market and far more profitable. In fact, the average mortgaged *short-term rental home*[2] in the United States generates six times more profits than the stock market, and a long-term rental produces three times more.[3] And since 1950, the stock market has lost 20 percent or more of its value a dozen times,[4] compared to only once for housing values.[5]

A *third sign* that you are a good candidate to be a real estate investor is a willingness to roll up your sleeves and do a little work. Passive investments like the stock market require little effort. Executives who sit at desks all day love the stock market (*at least when its value is up*).

A rental property requires a little more of your time. But I spend no more than 15 hours a week (often less) on both of my rental properties. The biggest part of my job is cleaning between guests at my short-term rental home. Of course, you can hire someone to do that, but when you do it yourself, you know it'll be done right, and there are big rewards for doing that. As of this writing, all 57 of the reviews I've received from Airbnb guests and 24 of 25 from Vrbo are 5-star (one 4-star from Vrbo).

For my efforts, I estimate that I earn about $62 an hour.[6] If I were

---

[2] A short-term rental is usually defined as a lease that lasts less than 28-30 days. In many states, guests must pay sales tax and other taxes on short-term stays.

[3] More details in Chapter 3.

[4] Mark Fonville, "Understanding Stock Market Corrections and Crashes," Covenant Wealth Advisors (2022), retrieved 7/25/23 from <www.covenantwealthadvisors.com/post/understanding-stock-market-corrections-and-crashes>.

[5] U.S. Census Bureau and U.S. Department of Housing and Urban Development, "Median Sales Price of Houses Sold for the United States [MSPUS]" (August 11, 2023), retrieved 8/12/23 from <https://fred.stlouisfed.org/series/MSPUS>.

[6] This figure is calculated by dividing my total profits in 2023 ($48,792; see Footnote 50) by 780 hours (15 hours a week × 52 weeks).

working full time, I would be earning an annual salary of $124,800. But unlike salaried workers, I pay little or no federal income tax on my rental income,[7] and so I save about $30,000 in taxes (federal income tax, social security, Medicaid and Medicare), which means I actually earn about $74 an hour.

There also are several good nonfinancial reasons why real estate is a great investment. *First*, you don't have to quit your regular job. You can work on your property when you're not working your regular job. *Second*, you don't need a college education or a real estate license. It's not rocket science, and you can learn as you go and reading about real estate in books and online, and by talking with other landlords, real estate agents, and friends. *Third*, you don't need a lot of money to invest, especially if you're a first-time home buyer. Several government-backed programs allow you to buy a home for less than 10 percent down. The U.S. Department of Veterans Affairs even has a no down-payment program. You can lease the home a year after you live in it.

If you can't afford the down payment, there are other options, and I explore them in this book. They include finding partners or investors, including friends or family members.

Purpose of This Book

The purpose of this book is to help you obtain your first rental house or convert your current home into one and achieve financial freedom as you define it. It's not as difficult as you might think.

If you already own a property, whether it's mortgaged or not, your job is easy. All you need to do is find other living arrangements for at least six months. You can stay with a friend or family member, or, if you

---

[7] I am drawing Social Security, but it is not counted as earned income.

have the resources, rent a cheaper place. After that, you can use the income on your rental property to obtain another mortgage, such as a DSCR loan,[8] to purchase another home for yourself or another rental property. That's what I did.

If you don't own a property but have a steady income, a good credit rating and not too much debt, you likely can qualify for a conventional mortgage loan or even a low-interest, low-down-payment mortgage loan through the Federal Housing Administration (FHA), Veterans Affairs (VA), or other government-backed loan programs.[9] As noted above, most require you to live in the house for at least a year, but after that you can rent it out.

Or you can forgo real estate investing altogether and spend the rest of your life working for someone else. (*Okay, maybe that isn't as bad as I just implied.*)

Either way, it can't hurt to learn more about investing in rental properties, even if you don't buy one. This knowledge can help you make better decisions when you buy a home for personal use as well.

Overview of Book

In Chapter 2, I'll show you how I achieved financial freedom through my three rental properties. I also show you how I used the equity in my house to turn it into a short-term rental. I do this not to brag but to give you ideas that can help you if you become a landlord or add to your portfolio.

The rest of the book is divided into seven parts.

---

[8]A Debt-Service Coverage Ratio mortgage loan is based not on your earned income but on the income you generate from your rental. See Chapter 21 for more details.

[9]The U.S. Department of Housing and Urban Development, which oversees the FHA, also provides mortgage loans tailored to the needs of Native Americans.

Part I shows you how much more profitable rental real estate is than the stock market and why. The forecasting model I create is based on 52 years of housing and stock market data and shows that the average $300,000 short-term rental home produces six times more profits than the stock market. A long-term rental generates three times more.

Leverage is the main reason real estate crushes stocks. Much of the profit that a rental property makes over time comes from appreciation. Homes almost always go up in value because historically there has always been a shortage of housing in America. And when you borrow other people's money to buy a home, you earn appreciation not just on the amount you put down, *but on the money you borrowed.*

There are lots of so-called real estate experts out there who pooh-pooh real estate rental investing. Don't listen to them. Many are trying to get you to invest in their Real Estate Investment Trust (REIT) funds or apartment complexes. But these investments typically perform even worse than the stock market (see Chapter 3), which historically has generated a modest 7.5 percent annualized gain.

In contrast, my short-term rental home produces a 121 percent annualized gain (this includes estimated appreciation). The average $300,000 rental home with a 3.5 percent down payment produces a gain of 263 percent. And these estimates are conservative. They are based on mortgage interest rates of 9.25 and 7 percent, respectively, as well as conservative estimates of profits and liberal estimates of costs.

Another reason not to listen to the critics is the popularity of landlordship. More than 14 million individuals own and lease property in the United States.[10] There are 129 million housing units in the United

---

[10]This figure excludes large corporations, which own most of the rental properties in the United States. See Drew DeSilver, "As National Eviction Ban Expires, a Look at Who Rents and Who Owns in the U.S.," Pew Research Center (August 2, 2021), retrieved 1/20/24 from <https://www.pewresearch.org/short-reads/2021/08/02/as-national-eviction-ban-expires-a-look-at-who-rents-and-who-owns-in-the-u-s>.

States, 82 million of which are homes.[11] A third of those units, about 43 million, are rentals. So if owning a rental property were less profitable than investing in stocks and REITs, why do so many individuals own rentals?

Parts II and III show you how to tap your assets to raise the money for a down payment to purchase a rental property. Your assets include your job, your home (if you own one), your autos and other valuables, and your friends, family, and outside investors. As noted above, if you have never had a mortgage and have a modest income, you likely can qualify for a low down payment and low-interest loan through one of many federally backed programs. I provide a brief summary of each of these programs.

Part IV shows you how to create a real estate business, even though you don't need to create one. You can operate as a sole proprietorship. But most entrepreneurs create a limited liability company (LLC) or a partnership, both of which can help protect your personal assets should you be sued.

Part V shows you how to buy a good rental property. The single most important rule is to buy in a good market. A good market helps ensure that your property appreciates in value over time. Before a mortgage is paid off, appreciation is the single biggest source of profits.

You also want to buy in a good market because they attract good guests and tenants. I also show you how to calculate your cash flow and estimate profits on your rental before you buy. If you can't turn a profit

---

[11]Statista, "U.S. Single Family Homes -Statistics & Facts," Statista (December 18, 2023), retrieved 1/19/24 from <https://www.statista.com/topics/5144/single-family-homes-in-the-us/#topicOverview>.

renting your property long term, don't buy, because if your short-term plan fails, you could lose your shirt.

Part VI shows you how to manage long- and short-term rentals and how to do your books and file your taxes. If you have a long-term rental, you must screen your tenants. That is the best way to ensure you get good ones.

I'll also show how to set up a short-term rental through Airbnb or Vrbo. The nice thing about short-term rentals is that you always get paid, because the guests are billed in advance.

Doing your books isn't difficult if you only have a couple of properties. Filing your taxes also is easy if you use a software program like TurboTax.

In Part VII, I show you how to buy your next rental even though you may not have enough cash on hand for a down payment. I purchased a condo by taking out a Debt-Service Coverage Ratio (DSCR) loan, which is based on the income you generate from your rental property, not your earned income. I'll also show you how to increase your rental rates without losing tenants and how to cut costs to increase your profits.

The appendix contains three tables that provide detailed information about how I calculated the profit estimates on three different properties: (1) my short-term rental, (2) a typical $300,000 home with a 7 percent mortgage and a 25 percent down payment, and (3) a $300,000 home with a 3.5 percent down payment and a 7 percent interest rate. These models include four sources of income and five categories of expenses, and profits on these three different properties are estimated over 10 years.

How I Became Financially Free

In 2020, I was in a financial pickle.

A recent divorce meant I was now paying all of the bills for my myself and my daughter, who was in college. I also owed my ex-wife $35,000 for her share in the Phoenix home that I had purchased with my retirement funds several years earlier.

My Social Security check and ghostwriting income weren't enough to cover all expenses. I retired earlier than I should have from my tenured teaching position at a Pac 10 university, partly because of an eight-year-long free speech legal battle with my administrators. I eventually won the landmark case,[12] but the federal appeals court refused to force the university to pay my attorney's fees, citing a controversial legal doctrine that exempts public institutions from liability even when they violate people's constitutional rights.

This was one of those *life-isn't-fair moments.*

You know what I'm talking about.

But griping wouldn't solve my financial dilemma. Instead, I decided to *tap my assets* (borrow on the equity in my home) and purchase a

---

[12]*Demers v. Austin*, 746 F.3d 402 (9th Circuit, January 29, 2014). For details, see David Demers, *Adventures of a Quixotic Professor: How One Man's Lifelong Passion for Social Justice Bristles Bureaucracies and Sparks a Landmark Free Speech Ruling* (Phoenix: Marquette Books, 2021).

condominium (where I could live) that allowed me to turn my home into a short-term rental investment property.

Risky?

A little.

But far less dicey than investing in the stock market or flipping homes. I knew this because at the time I was ghostwriting a book titled *ABCs of Buying Rental Property* for Scottsdale real estate investor Ken McElroy.[13] I had read his previous books and had done a fair amount of research on real estate investing.[14]

Ken was right: Real estate rentals are a far better and safer investment than either the stock market or flipping.[15] In fact, I even produced quantitative evidence for this claim in his book, which I've updated and refined even more in the book you are now reading (*we'll get to that in Chapters 3 and 4*).

My First Rental (Condo in Sun City, AZ)

Back to my story.

In July 2019, I secured a $180,000 conventional cash-out refinance mortgage loan on my Phoenix home and purchased a $139,000 rental condominium in Sun City, Arizona.[16] Sun City is a vacation destination

---

[13]Ken McElroy, *ABCs of Buying Rental Property: How You Can Achieve Financial Freedom in Five Years* (Scottsdale: RDA Press, 2020). The book was the sixth-best seller in the category "real estate investing and finance." The book lost some of its ranking, though, in 2023, because a second printing (updated design, same publication date), but it continues to climb the rankings. As of this writing, it was #13.

[14]You can find a promotional video for the book featuring an interview between Ken and me at <https://www.youtube.com/watch?v=a5RExfeU4UY&t=605s>.

[15]When a corporation goes bankrupt, stockholders can lose everything. But a rental property rarely loses all of its value, because people always need a place to live and there is a shortage of housing in America.

[16]The rest of the loan was used to pay off my ex-wive's $35,000 debt and closing costs on the purchase. At that time, Sun City collected a $3,500 recreation fee for every home sale. Now the fee is more than $4,000.

for people 55 or older, especially those living in northern states who want to replace the cold and snow with sunshine and palm trees.

I did a few repairs on the condo and then posted it for rent on Vrbo (Vacation Rentals by Owner). Within weeks, the place was booked for the next seven months and would generate more than $15,000 in gross revenue, which is more than twice as much as my mortgage payments.

Then COVID hit.

All of my future guests canceled their bookings.

But instead of grousing, I stuck a "For Rent" sign in the front yard and leased the condo to local residents for another 15 months. I covered my expenses and sold the property in April 2021 for $185,000. I walked away with nearly $59,000 in profits (appreciation and rental income) — not bad for a 22-month investment in the middle of COVID.[17]

I repaid the cash-out refinance mortgage loan on my home, gave my daughter my 2018 Corolla, and purchased a low-mileage 2017 Camry for myself. The only major debt I had now was a small monthly payment on my car. But I still needed a bigger financial cushion.

My Second Rental (Home in Phoenix)

So a year later I converted my North Phoenix home into a short-term rental. I reasoned that if my Sun City property could survive COVID, surely my 1,920-square-foot middle-class home, which featured a very large (15-by-35-foot) heated swimming pool, could do even better.

I loved my home, but my daughter was away at college and I didn't need a place that big. So I moved in with a friend and about a month

---

[17] I didn't have to pay capital gains on the sale because my taxable earned income was low (well below $41,675). However, taxpayers normally will pay 15 percent on capital gains if their income is between $41,676 and $459,750, and 20 percent above that. James Royal, "What Is the Long-Term Capital Gains Tax," Bankrate (March 10, 2023), retrieved 6/16/23 from <https://www.bankrate.com/ investing/long-term-capital-gains-tax>.

later, in mid-June 2022, I listed my house for rent on both Airbnb and Vrbo. My biggest concern was whether guests would come during the summer, when temperatures in Phoenix often exceed 110 degrees.

I priced it competitively at $99 a night (minimum three-night stay and $75 cleaning fee) for the summer months, which was slightly higher than the cheap one-room motels on I-17 a half-mile away. In the headlines for the postings, I framed the property as "A Good Value for the Money." The first picture in the postings featured my swimming pool, adorned with a couple of colorful floating toys.[18]

I slowly increased rental rates through the fall and into December. I set the rates at $179 in January and February of 2023 and $199 in March, which are peak tourist months in Phoenix. I charged a premium for the six nights around February 12 ($600 to $1,000 a night), when the Chiefs played the Eagles in the Super Bowl at State Farm Stadium in Glendale, about 14 miles away.

My rental calendar filled up. Three of the five first renters each leased one of the three peak months, which generated gross revenues of $5,100, $7,200 and $5,300, respectively. To my delight, the summer schedule also filled up. People do visit Phoenix in the summer, often to see family or friends or attend a wedding or other event. Of course, if they have to come to Phoenix in the blazing hot summer, they want a swimming pool to cool them down.

I increased the rates about one-third after April 2023. I was a bit nervous about that. Would guests still come?

They did.

In fact, by the end of April 2023, about three-fourths of the days between then and December 2023 were booked.

I grossed $16,219 in rental income during the first six months (from

---

[18]Here is the link to my rental home listing at Airbnb <https://airbnb.com/h/davessunshinegetaway>.

June to December 2022) even though I only rented the property for four and a half of those months (I blocked out six weeks for personal use). That averaged out to $3,600 a month, nearly $1,400 more than I would have received renting it via a long-term lease (6 months or more). Other sources of income included $23,000 in appreciation on the property[19] and $150 in depreciation tax savings.[20] My total gross income was $39,469 and my total expenses were $11,717, which meant the property generated a profit of $27,652 in 2022.

Not bad for the first six months.

But I had one more financial problem to solve before I could join the financial freedom club. I needed to find an affordable apartment for my daughter, who would return to Phoenix in spring 2023 after completing her master's in education at the University of Arizona in Tucson. She would eventually secure a good job teaching mathematics at a Phoenix area high school.

My Third Rental (Condo in Phoenix)

I began the search for an apartment for my daughter in early November 2022. But after two weeks it became clear that monthly rental rates for an apartment in a decent, safe area of the city were just too high. The going rate was about $2,000 a month — an amount that would consume more than half of her expected net salary after taxes.

She couldn't afford that.

---

[19]My house was valued at $420,000 in January 2022, according to Zillow, and $460,000 in December 2022, according to an appraisal commissioned by my lending institution (a 9.5% increase). For this analysis, I used a more conservative 5 percent increase, which is roughly the average yearly rate of increase for homes in the United States. See Notes to Appendix 1 for details.

[20]Depreciation allows you to deduct the cost of a capital asset, like a home or a refrigerator, over a period of time under the assumption that it wears out. See Text Box 2.1 for more details.

Text Box 2.1 – What Is Depreciation?

Depreciation allows you to deduct the cost of a capital asset, like a home or a refrigerator, over a period of time under the assumption that it wears out. The IRS treats depreciation as an expenditure. But real estate investors often think of it as a source of income, because it can reduce your tax bill at the end of the year. Let me explain.

When you buy something for a business you own and manage, such as office supplies, the Internal Revenue Service allows you to deduct the entire cost of the supplies from the income you make in the business during that year. That usually lessens your tax burden. Those items represent the cost of doing business and usually are quickly consumed.

For more expensive items, the law forces you to deduct the cost more slowly. The deduction for most rental homes is taken over 27.5 years, or roughly 1/27.5 each year (3.64 percent per year). So if you bought your property for $100,000, you get to deduct about $3,640 from your earned income that year. If your income is higher than about $45,000 and less than $95,000, that amounts to about a 22 percent savings on your tax bill, or about $800 ($3,640 × 22% = $801).

Depreciation lessens the chances of fraud. If it didn't exist, a real estate investor could buy a property, take a $100,000 tax deduction that year, and then declare bankruptcy. This essentially would amount to a transfer of wealth from taxpayers to investors. To complicate things even more, the logic of depreciation (that things wear out over time) doesn't usually apply to real property, at least in the first 100 to 200 years or so in the life of the property. Rental properties usually appreciate over time. So you don't lose money, you make money.

Of course, the IRS knows this, and when your property appreciates in value more than what you paid for it, you may have to pay a capital gains tax (15% or 20%) when you sell it (see Chapter 4). In addition, you likely will have to pay a 25 percent depreciation recapture tax on the amount you wrote off during the years you owned the property. There are some exceptions, and I'll discuss them and the general issue of taxes in Chapters 20 and 21.

Besides, paying rent is such a waste of money. All of the tax benefits of property ownership go to wealthy apartment landlords, who had already raised rental rates in Phoenix by more than 40 percent during the previous three years.[21] So I pivoted to the idea of buying a condo and leasing part of it to her at a reduced rate — a win-win for both of us.[22]

The only obstacle was whether I could qualify for a mortgage loan. Even though I had no debts and was making money on my rental home, my earned income was low because of the generous tax write-offs on my rental property (interest on the mortgage, depreciation, insurance, taxes, maintenance costs, and utilities — topics I'll explore later).

In short, *cash flow* was my problem,[23] and it's a problem that confronts most small-time landlords after they buy their first rental. They can't qualify for another conventional loan because the depreciation and other deductions on their rentals wipe out much of their earned income. Unfortunately, conventional banks and lending institutions don't care about the equity that is generated through appreciation and principal payments. They focus narrowly on earned income, because they want their loans secured by the federal government. This means they have no risk when they finance a property.[24] *Wouldn't that be nice if the rest of*

---

[21]The increase occurred from 2019 to 2022. See "Phoenix, AZ Rental Market Trend," Apartment List (June 2023), retrieved 6/25/23 from <https://www.apartmentlist.com/rent-report/az/phoenix>.

[22]You can live in a home or condo and lease it, too. You must report the income and can only deduct about half of the expenses.

[23]Cash flow is defined as money flowing into and out of a business. Positive cash flow is often used synonymously with profit, but not necessarily. See Chapter 14.

[24]When loans are secured by the federal government, lending institutions essentially have no risk, and taxpayers foot the bill when something catastrophic occurs. That was the case in 2008, when a financial crisis caused in large part by the lenders themselves led to $16 billion in losses that taxpayers were forced to cover. See Tad Dehaven, "Corporate Welfare in the Federal Government," *Policy Analysis*, 703 (July 25, 2012), pp. 6–7, retrieved 7/20/23, from <https://www.google.com/url?sa=t&rct=j&q=&esrc=s&source=web&cd=&cad=rja&uact=8&ved=2ahUKEwiL9qmmhvH_AhWWJkQIHSZHA344HhAWegQIAhAB&url=https%3A%2F%2Fwww.realclearmarkets.com%2Fblog%2FPA703.pdf&usg=AOvVaw3LClmvEZ4JtWFbcCRVh7ul&opi=89978449>.

us had the same privilege?

Fortunately, the private commercial lending industry has come up with a solution to the cash-flow problem. It's call a Debt-Service Coverage Ratio (DSCR) loan, which doesn't care about how much earned income you have. It cares only about the income you make on your rental property. To qualify, you need at least six months of rental income and usually some equity on your property to secure the loan. By December 2022, my rental home met those criteria.

I contacted several private lenders, all of whom were willing to loan me money to purchase another rental property. So in mid-November 2022, I switched from looking for apartments to looking for condos.

In terms of reasonably priced condos, there wasn't much available in Phoenix, because home sales had declined substantially. The stock market had lost about 30 percent of its value from December 2021 to September 2022,[25] and the inflation rate was nearly 10 percent.[26] Mortgage rates had more than doubled, to 7 percent or higher.[27] During such times, people cling to their properties because they can't obtain a mortgage interest rate comparable to or lower than their current rate.

But I eventually found a one-story, two-bedroom, two-bath condo in a 400-unit complex in north Phoenix for $260,000. An inspection (always get one) revealed that the flexible air ducts in the attic were deteriorating because of a defective design, but the company was no longer reimbursing buyers for the problem. I counter-offered with

---

[25]"S&P 500 Index – 90 Year Historical Chart," Macrotrends (June 23, 2023), retrieved 6/25/23, from <https://www.macrotrends.net/2324/sp-500-historical-chart-data>.

[26]Russ Wiles, "Metro Phoenix Inflation Rate Dips to 8.5%, But Is Still Among Mation's Hotspots,"*Arizona Republic* (March 14, 2023), retrieved 6/25/23, from <https://www.azcentral.com/story/money/business/economy/2023/03/14/ inflation-drops-slightly-in-metro-phoenix-still-among-highest-in-us/70007523007>.

[27]Sabrina Karl, "Mortgage Rates' September Surge Continues, Hitting a Level not Seen in 20 Years," Investopedia (September 28, 2022), retrieved 6/25/22, from <https://www.investopedia.com/today-s-mortgage-rates-and-trends-september-28-2022-rates-soar-6744762>.

$250,000 and the seller accepted.[28] We signed a purchase agreement in early December. I borrowed $285,000 to cover the purchase, which included closing costs, and closed on the DSCR loan in late December.

As expected, the interest rate was high (9.25%), partly because such loans are not guaranteed by taxpayers.

But don't let high interest rates freak you out. Novice investors tend to focus too much on cash flow (gross rental income – expenditures) and not enough on the other three sources of income (appreciation, equity from principal, and depreciation), which collectively usually contribute more to profits than rental income alone, especially before the mortgage is paid off. Interest rates are important, but don't let them fully dictate your decision to purchase. The key is whether you can turn a profit, and I'll show you how to estimate that for a typical rental home in Chapter 3 and for your proposed property in Chapter 15.

I closed on the condo on January 3, 2023. I deliberately pushed the closing date into 2023 for tax purposes, because I already had enough write-offs in 2022.

I spruced up and furnished the property in January and rented it in February and March, which generated $5,881 in revenue. I moved into the condo in late March.

Three months later my daughter moved in. I charged her $1,200 for rent and utilities, about half of what she would normally have had to pay to live in an apartment.

During 2023, the Phoenix condo generated $14,281 in gross rent and $9,388 in appreciation. Expenses were $4,150 plus $5,455 in depreciation. For tax purposes, my reported net income on the property was $4,676. But my actual profit on the property, after taking appreciation into account, was $23,669.

---

[28]Fortunately, I didn't have to pay for the repairs. The condo homeowners association took responsibility.

Figure 2.1
2019-23 Income, Profits & Expenses on My Rentals

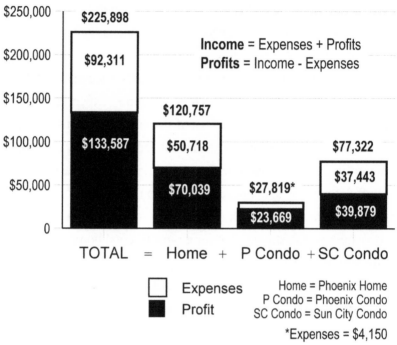

Figure 2.1 above sums up the income, profits, and expenses on my three rentals.

My Bottom Line (Financial Freedom)

From 2019 to 2023, my three properties generated $225,898 in revenue, which includes rental income, appreciation, equity from principal payments, and tax savings from depreciation. My expenses — which included mortgage payments, landlord insurance, property taxes, repairs and maintenance, and utilities — were $92,311. This yielded a profit of $133,587 ($225,898 − $92,311).

The property generating the most profits was my short-term rental home ($70,039). As noted earlier in this chapter, during the first 6½ months of 2022, it generated a profit of $27,652. In 2023, the house generated a profit of $42,387 (see Appendix 1 for details).

My Phoenix condo turned in the highest profit rate ($23,699 on a gross income of $27,819, or 85%). It was rented for three-fourths of the year and generated only $4,150 in expenses, because there is no mortgage on the property.[29]

My Sun City property was rented for 22 months and generated $39,879 in profits on a total gross income of $77,322.

One additional comment about my short-term rental home. I bought the property in 2014 for $159,000. As of this writing, it is worth $460,000. That's an 11 percent *annualized* increase (see Text Box 2.2). But I used a conservative 5 percent annualized increase to calculate the appreciation over the next 10 years. Had I used an 11 percent estimate, my total profit from appreciation would be $846,134 instead of $289,291. So my total profit on the property would have been more than $1.1 million instead of $572,843. My original investment was $35,000, so that's a phenomenal 3,143 percent *return on investment*.[30]

"GROOVY," as my generation used to say.

In Chapter 3, I explain in detail how I obtained these numbers and how to estimate profits for an average property in the United States. You can use this information to create your own estimates (see Chapter 15). Although there are no guarantees when it comes to investing, when you

---

[29]The mortgage loan is tied to my Phoenix home, so that property takes the write-offs. This can also be viewed as a business loan, in the sense that it enabled me to buy the condo. For tax purposes, though, it doesn't matter which property writes off the loan, because both are reported on Schedule E.

[30]The formula for calculating return on investment (ROI) is simply the percent-change formula you learned in junior high school ([New Value – Old Value] ÷ Old Value).The formula can be simplified even more: ROI = Profit ÷ Cost of the Investment. Multiply the ratio by 100 to turn it into a percent change.

Text Box 2.2 – What Is Annualized Gain?

Annualized gain (or loss) means that the interest gains or losses on an asset or investment are compounded as each year passes.

So let's say you invest $1,000 and the interest rate is 10 percent a year. At the beginning of year two you will have $1,100 ($1,000 + [$1,000 × 10%]). At the end of year two, the amount is $1,210, not $1,200, because the interest earned at year one ($100) also is multiplied by 10%, adding another $10 to the total ($1,000 + [$1,100 × 10%). Thus, when interest is compounded, investments grow at a faster pace.

The simple way to calculate annualized gain is to use an online compound interest calculator (the hand formula is too complicated for compounding over years). Enter the starting value of a property ($100,000) and the number of years (10). Then adjust the interest rate until the final figure is close to the ending value of the property ($150,000). In this case, the annualized return is 4 percent.

Here is the formula for those who like math: Divide 150,000 by 100,000 to get 1.5. Then apply to 1.5 the exponent 1/10 to get 1.04. Subtract 1 to get 0.04, then multiply by 100, which is 4 percent.

do your research, you are in a much better position to reduce risk and make good decisions.

In Chapter 4, I'll explain why profits on rental homes crush stock market returns.

Part I
Rental Real Estate Crushes Stocks

How Much More Profitable Are Rentals?

Commentaries and articles on business and investing websites often claim that stocks produce higher returns than real estate. Here are some recent examples.

"Historically, the stock market experiences higher growth than the real estate market, making it a better way to grow your money."
        –Investopedia (July 27, 2022)[31]

"[S]tock market returns generally outperform real estate investments by a significant amount over the long run..."
        –*Yahoo.com* (January 23, 2023)[32]

"[H]istorically, stocks have offered better returns than real estate investments. 'Stocks have returned, on average, about 8% to 12% per year while real estate has generated returns of 2% to 4% per year.'"
        –*U.S. News & World Report* (May 30, 2023)[33]

---

[31]Sean Ross, "Has Real Estate or the Stock Market Performed Better Historically?" Investopedia (July 27, 2022), retrieved 7/14/23, from <www.investopedia.com/ask/answers/052015/which-has-performed-better-historically-stock-market-or-real-estate.asp>.

[32]John Csiszar, "Should You Invest in Real Estate or the Stock Market?" Yahoo.com (Jan. 23, 2023), retrieved 7/14/23, from <https://www.yahoo.com/ now/invest-real-estate-stock-market-120027283.html>.

[33]Alani Asis, "Real Estate vs. Stocks: Which Has Higher Returns?" *U.S. News & World Report* (May 30, 2023), retrieved 7/12/23, from <https://money.usnews.com/ investing/articles/real-estate-vs-stocks-which-has-higher-returns>.

A recent *MarketWatch* article even discouraged investors from becoming landlords and instead encouraged them to buy into Real Estate Investment Trusts,[34] which pool investors' monies to fund commercial real estate ventures. The article claimed that REITs were generating 12 percent average annualized returns (see Text Box 2.2 for definition).

But I analyzed the data and found that from 1995 to 2023 the average annualized gain for the eight REIT funds listed in the article was only 6 percent.[35] This was even less than the annualized gains for the S&P 500, which were 6.4 percent over the same period.[36]

Investing in the stock market has many advantages. It's easy to do and requires little time and expense, especially if you don't use a broker. It's also *liquid*, meaning you can pull your money out at any time. But when it comes to generating profits, one thing is indisputable: RENTAL REAL ESTATE CRUSHES STOCKS. And I'll prove it. I'll compare profits from the S&P 500 Index to the profits for a typical rental home or condo.

Profit Estimates for the S&P 500

From 1970 to 2022, the S&P 500 grew in value from 92 to 3,840, which is an average annualized gain of 7.5 percent.[37]

---

[34]Brett Arends, "Don't Become a Landlord — Own These REITs Instead," *Marketwatch* (July 5, 2023), retrieved 7/12/23, from <www.marketwatch.com/ story/dont-be-a-landlordown-these-reits-instead-158e7923>.

[35]I became suspicious of the data because I had invested in REITs before and discovered their returns were no better than the stock market.

[36]The story asserted that from1995 to 2023 REITs increased 2,000 percent and home values 300 percent. The REITs actually increased 551 percent, compared to 301 percent for home values (this latter value was accurate). But real estate is still much more profitable because gains from appreciation are calculated on not just the money that is put down on the property but also the money borrowed through a mortgage. This is called leverage and I address it in Chapter 4.

[37]Macrotrends, retrieved 6/8/23, from <https://www.macrotrends.net/ 2324/sp-500-historical-chart-data>. I excluded dividends from profits because dividend values are already built into stock prices. Claire Boyte-White, "How Dividends Affect Stock Prices With Examples," *Investopedia* (August 29, 2023), retrieved 12/23/23 from

Figure 3.1

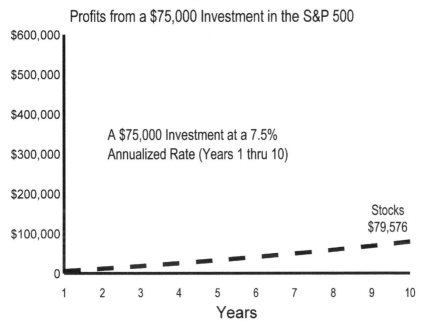

Profits from a $75,000 Investment in the S&P 500

A $75,000 Investment at a 7.5%
Annualized Rate (Years 1 thru 10)

Stocks
$79,576

Years

If you invested $75,000 in the stock market, a year later you would have a profit of $5,625 ($75,000 × 7.5%). Ten years later, your profit would grow to $79,576 (see Figure 3.1 above). This is a return on investment (ROI) of 106 percent ($79,576 ÷ $75,000).[38]

A 7.5 percent annualized gain is a decent return. It's greater than the inflation rate, which is usually around 3 percent. An investment at 7 percent roughly doubles in size every 10 years.

I chose a long (52-year) time period to create these profit-rate estimates, because stock values are often volatile. In fact, since 1950, the stock market has lost more than 20 percent of its value on a dozen occasions.

<https://www.investopedia.com/articles/investing/091015/how-dividends-affect-stock-prices.asp>. Even if the dividends are added, real estate is still much more profitable.

[38]Return on investment (ROI) measures the amount of return on an investment relative to the investment's cost. See footnote 30 for details.

To make reasonably accurate forecasts about future values of stocks as well as housing prices, a stable average is needed. The beginning date selected for a time period has a big effect on the annualized gain. If one selects a starting point during an extreme down or up period, the average growth rate likely will be distorted.

After examining growth statistics for the stock and housing markets, I chose the time period between 1970 and 2022. Housing and market prices were relatively stable in 1970, and 52 years is long enough to smooth out the ups and downs.

I also selected the S&P 500 to represent the stock market, rather than the Dow Jones Industrial Average, for two reasons. First, the S&P is composed of more companies (500 v. 30), which produces a more stable result over time. Second, the S&P index uses a more accurate method of assessing market value than the Dow.[39]

The upshot is that the S&P index produces a decent return for investors. But is 7.5 percent better than a typical rental property?

No. It's not even close.

Profit Estimates for a Typical Rental Home

A typical short-term rental home or condo with a market value of $300,000 and a 7 percent 30-year fixed mortgage produces an average annualized return of 21.6 percent, which is nearly three times greater than the S&P 500. With a $75,000 down payment (same as the stock investor), the investment will generate a $41,049 profit in the first year and will grow to $531,074 in 10 years, which is six times greater than the

---

[39]The S&P 500 is market weighted, unlike the Dow. But either index produces similar results for this analysis. See "Which Stock Market Index Is Better To Track? The Dow or S&P 500 Index," Greenbush Financial (not dated), retrieved 7/24/23 from <https://www.greenbushfinancial.com/all-blogs/which-stock-market-index-is-better-to-track-the-dow-or-sp-500-index>.

Figure 3.2

Profits from an Average House Rental vs. Stocks

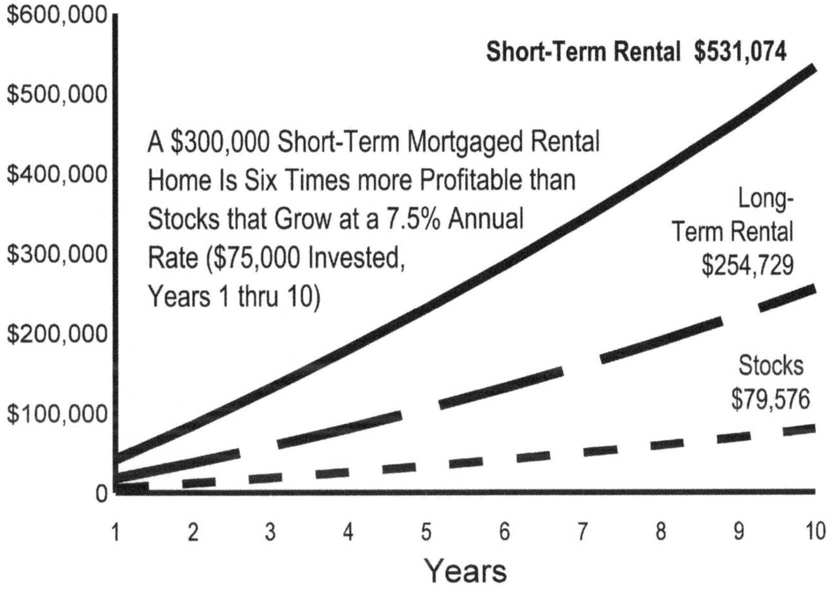
$600,000
$500,000
$400,000
$300,000
$200,000
$100,000
0
Short-Term Rental $531,074
A $300,000 Short-Term Mortgaged Rental Home Is Six Times more Profitable than Stocks that Grow at a 7.5% Annual Rate ($75,000 Invested, Years 1 thru 10)
Long-Term Rental $254,729
Stocks $79,576
1 2 3 4 5 6 7 8 9 10
Years

stock market (see Figure 3.2) and a whopping 708 percent return on investment ($531,074 ÷ $75,000).

A long-rental generates less profits than a short-term rental, but the return is still three times greater than the stock market. In the first year, the long-term rental generates $17,775 in profits compared to $5,625 for the stock market. At the end of 10 years, the long-term rental returns $254,729 in profits, a 340 percent ROI.

Are you skeptical?

Good.

Because now I'll show you how I calculated those numbers, which, by the way, are conservative. I overestimated inflationary costs over time and underestimated inflation's effects on income. In addition, if mortgage interest rates drop below 7 percent, profits on rental properties will increase even more.

How I Calculated Profits on a Typical Rental Home

To derive profit statistics for a typical rental property in America, I first found the median value of a typical home in America.[40] Census data showed that it was about $480,000 in 2023 — up considerably from previous years.[41]

But the average rental home isn't that expensive, partly because it's difficult turn a profit on a home with a high value. The national average rental rate for a 2-bedroom, 2-bath home is about $2,200 a month, according to Realtor.com.[42] A mortgage payment on a $400,000 home can easily exceed that amount.[43] That's partly why most rental homes are valued at less than $400,000.

So, for this analysis, I calculated the earnings on a $300,000 rental home with a $225,000 30-year fixed mortgage at 7 percent interest. Interest rates have been much lower in previous years, but in 2023 this was the national average. Mortgage interest rates on rental properties typically are slightly higher, because the lending industry considers them to be a higher risk. I used a 7 percent interest rate because I believe interest rates will decline in the coming months, and I don't want to provide estimates that are too expense-heavy. My estimates are still conservative, because I used a lower appreciation rate and calculated expenses using relatively high inflationary numbers (5% or more per year on all expenses).

---

[40] I could not find a source that provided the median value of a rental home.

[41] U.S. Census Bureau and U.S. Department of Housing and Urban Development, "Median Sales Price of Houses Sold for the United States" [MSPUS]), retrieved 6/8/23, from the Federal Reserve Bank of St. Louis <https://fred.stlouisfed.org/series/MSPUS>).

[42] In July 2023, the average national rental rate for a two-bedroom apartment was about $2,000. See "July 2023 Rental Report: Rents Fall for the Third Month in a Row," Realtor.com, retrieved 8/22/23 from <https://www.realtor.com/research/july-2023-rent>.

[43] A $300,000 mortgage at 7 percent interest produces a monthly payment of nearly $2,400 with taxes and insurance.

Appendix 2 provides the year-by-year details on the sources of income and expenses for this typical $300,000 home. The resources I used to calculate these estimates are contained in the footnotes to Appendix 2.

Income on a $300,000 Rental Home

There are four major sources of income on a rental home: (1) rental income (short- or long-term), (2) appreciation, (3) principal pay down (or equity from principal), and (4) depreciation. Figure 3.3 on the next page shows those four sources on a short-term rental.

Total gross income is estimated at $70,812. The lion's share comes from rental income, which is estimated at $52,800, or $4,400 a month (see column D in Appendix 2). This is twice as much as would be expected with a long-term lease ($2,200).

Appreciation provides the next largest source of income ($15,000). This figure is based on an average 5 percent annualized gain, which is slightly lower than the actual historical average of 5.9 percent (see Chapter 2).

The other two sources of income are much smaller. When you make the mortgage payments, some of the proceeds pay off the principal on the loan. As you probably know, the amounts are small in the early years of a mortgage. Most of the mortgage payment goes to pay off the interest. Nevertheless, after one year, this average rental property will generate $2,286 in principal equity.

The depreciation deduction on this property is about $8,727. The IRS treats depreciation as an expense, but real estate investors often see it as a source of income.[44] That's because it often lowers their tax bill at the end of the year. For example, if your earned income from other sources

---

[44]See Text Box 2.1 in Chapter 2.

Figure 3.3

First-Year Sources of Income from a $300,000 Short-Term Rental House

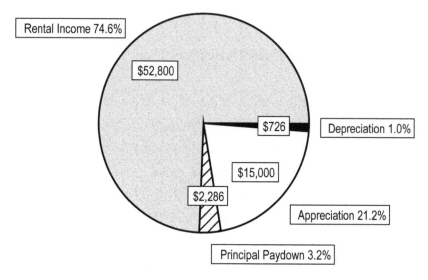

Total Income = $70,812

was between $44,726 and $95,375, you'd save about $2,000 in taxes.

But for this analysis I assumed that the only income is derived from the property itself, and because there are lots of other write-offs, your tax savings is only estimated at $726. There are no savings if you are renting on a long-term contract, because your gross income is even lower.

You need income to save on depreciation. But the depreciation deduction is not lost if you can't write it off in a particular year. The amount can be carried over to future years, when your income is higher. The depreciation write-offs continue to build as long as you don't use them.[45]

---

[45]Compare rows F and H in Table 4.1 in Chapter 4 to see the effects of depreciation on tax savings.

Figure 3.4

First-Year Expenses on $300,000 Short-Term Rental House

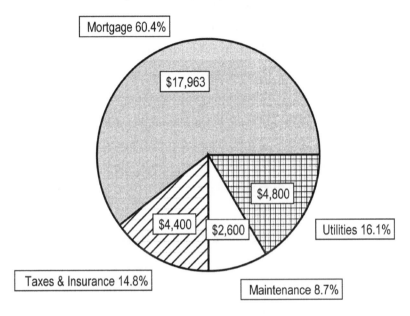

Mortgage 60.4%

$17,963

$4,800

$4,400 $2,600   Utilities 16.1%

Taxes & Insurance 14.8%

Maintenance 8.7%

Total Expenses= $29,763

Expenses on a $300,000 Rental Home

Appendix 2 (column G) shows that the mortgage payments on a $225,000 loan (principal and interest) are $17,963 a year, or $1,497 a month. That comprises about 60 percent of all of the expenses (see Figure 3.4) of a short-term rental.

In addition to the mortgage payment, the expenses on this home include property taxes and landlord insurance ($4,400), maintenance ($2,600), and utilities ($4,800). The latter is high because with a short-term rental the landlord must pay for internet service, electricity, and other utility expenses. With a long-term rental, these items are usually the responsibility of the tenant.

The upshot is that total expenses on a short-term rental are estimated at $29,763, compared to $70,812 in income. So, in the first year, the short-term rental property would produce a profit of $41,049. This includes appreciation of $15,000. When that is removed, the property generates a positive cash flow of $26,049. Now that's reasonable.

However, the long-term property only produces a positive cash flow of $2,775 when the $15,000 in appreciation is removed from gross income. If you don't have other income to cover unexpected costs, you might wait to purchase a rental property when the mortgage interest rates drop. That would then provide you with a better cash flow.

The Bottom Line for a Typical Rental Home

A typical short-term rental in the United States is about six times more profitable than the stock market and a long-term rental is three times more profitable. A short-term rental generates a comfortable cash flow of about $26,000, even with a $225,000 mortgage at 7 percent interest. A long-term rental, though, only generates about $2,700 per year, which is not a comfortable margin.

If the air conditioner had to be replaced, a landlord would have to cough up the difference. The long-term property is still appreciating at an average of $15,000 or more every year. But, unless the landlord had the supplemental income to cover a cash flow shortage, it might be better to wait to purchase a property when mortgage interest rates are lower.

Why Commentaries about Stocks Are Wrong

So why do so many commentaries and articles incorrectly assume that stocks generate higher returns than real estate rental properties?

Two main reasons.

A news bias and failure to do the math.

News Bias

Stories and commentaries about investing are heavily biased in favor of stocks and corporations. A Google search of the term "stock market news" produces 43.8 million mentions, compared to 594,000 for "real estate news," 528,000 for "bond market news," 78,300 for "precious metal news," 144,000 for "commodities market news," and 121,000 for "gold market news."[46]

The stock market dominates other segments of the investing world because it is more powerful, which means it has more effects on people, organizations, and communities. In America, more than 150 million adults — 61 percent of the population — own stocks, often through mutual funds, pensions and retirement funds, and annuity or insurance funds.[47] The value of those stocks is nearly $23 trillion.[48] In contrast, only about 14 million individuals are landlords, most of whom manage just one property.

Mass media sociologists point out that all mainstream business news is biased toward powerful organizations, institutions, and people, partly because these entities have more effects on the world and their communities. To see this process at work, just watch a couple of hours of broadcast television investment news on CNBC, Bloomberg, or Fox Business. They devote the majority of their coverage to discussions

---

[46]The analysis was conducted on August, 17, 2023.

[47]Jeffrey M. Jones, "What Percentage of Americans Own Stock?" Gallup News (May 24, 2023), retrieved 8/16/23 from <https://news.gallup.com/poll/266807/percentage-americans-owns-stock.aspx>.

[48]"Market Statistics — October 2021," World Federation of Exchanges (September 21, 2021), retrieved 1/26/24 from <https://focus.world-exchanges.org/issue/october-2021/market-statistics>.

about earnings and events that affect stock markets and corporations.

Of course, these networks also spend some time talking about real estate markets, bonds, precious metals, commodities, and financial markets. But the lion's share of coverage goes to stocks and corporations, because, again, this is where the vast majority of wealth and power in America is stashed.

Other non-broadcast business news organizations — such as *The Wall Street Journal, MarketWatch, Forbes* — also depend heavily on powerful corporations, both public and private, for news. This dependence manifests itself in a systemic and often subtle bias that promotes the welfare and interests of these entities.

This bias also is reflected in the proclamations of real estate entrepreneur Grant Cardone, who even argues that people should rent instead of buying a home because, he contends, home ownership is not a good investment (see Text Box 3.1 for more details).

The bottom line is that business news reinforces the well-documented proposition in social scientific research that *all media serve a master*.[49]

Failure to Do the Math

The second reason commentaries and stories wrongly assert that stocks produce higher returns than real estate rental investments is that the authors simply do not do the math. Most only compare annualized rates of return and stop there (7.5% v. 5.9%). They fail to look at rental income, appreciation generated from other people's money (leverage), and equity from principal payments. They don't even provide evidence

---

[49]For an in-depth and readable analysis of how the news media work, see Taehyun Kim, Dan Erickson, and David Demers, *How the Mass Media Really Work: An Introduction to Their Role as Institutions of Social Control and Change* (Spokane, WA: Marquette Books, 2014).

Text Box 3.1
Home Ownership Is a Good Investment
Here's Why Grant Cardone Is Wrong

In September 2023, *Moneywise*, which produces advertisement-infused news, published a story headlined "Grant Cardone says buying a home is a 'terrible investment.'"*

The controversial multimillionaire real estate entrepreneur argued that a home "is never going to pay you" and urged people to rent and invest their money into real estate stocks and other equity investments.

To defend his position, Cardone points out that homeowners pay a lot of mortgage interest and repairs and maintenance. But he fails to add that renters also pay these costs in their monthly payments and that homeowners benefit from leveraged appreciation.

In fact, using a half century of statistical data from the Census Bureau and other sources, a non-rental home will produce returns that are twice as high as the stock market and real estate investment trusts.**

From 1970 to 2022, the S&P 500 Index posted an average annualized gain of 7.5 percent per year. So if you invested $75,000 into the index, your profit during the first year would be $5,625 ($75,000 × 7.5%).

Home values increased an average of 5.9 percent from 1970 to 2022. So, if you had invested that money as a down payment on a $300,000 home, your appreciation on the property during the first year would be $15,000, nearly three times as much as stocks.

My analysis also shows that it is less costly to own and maintain a home with a 7 percent interest mortgage than to rent a similar property (about $400 less per month, $2,080 v. $2,500).

After 10 years, your home would generate a total of $188,669 in appreciation and $31,923 in equity from principal payments, while stocks would only produce a gain of $79,576. In sum, the home produced gains that were 2.7 times higher than the stock investments.

*The story is available at <https://moneywise.com/real-estate/grant-cardone-says-buying-a-house-is-a-terrible-investment>.

**For details, see my YouTube video at <https://youtu.be/56tXK_EN9aQ>.

to back up what they write. Many are stock brokers or fund managers who want you to buy their equity products.

The reality is that stocks will only beat rental real estate when all three of these conditions are met: (1) Real estate investors pay cash for their properties and refuse to mortgage them; (2) Real estate investors refuse to rent their properties, which denies them rental income; and (3) Stock investors put the same amount of money into the stock market as the real estate investor paid for the rental home.

But no real estate investors in their right minds would refuse to rent their property or mortgage it (unless they didn't care about maximizing their returns). As I pointed out in this chapter, savvy investors put as little down as they can on the purchase of a property so that they can leverage other people's money. This maximizes their profits and tax savings and frees up monetary assets for use on other projects, a topic we'll address in the next chapter.

Why Rental Real Estate Crushes Stocks

Recall from Chapter 2 that I invested $35,000 to obtain a $285,000 loan to purchase a condo so I could continue to rent my home property, which was valued at $460,000.

My home generated a profit of $42,387 during its first full year of operation (2023). My expenses were $39,001 and my gross income, which includes appreciation, was $81,388 ($81,388 – $39,001 = $42,387; for details, see Appendix 1, year 1).[50]

Now let's compare that to the S&P 500, which climbed from a value of 3,824 to 4,770 in 2023 — a gain or return on investment of 25 percent in one year. That's much faster than the normal yearly gain of 7.5 percent. The economy was rebounding in 2023 after an inflationary period caused in part by the COVID pandemic of 2020 and profiteering businesses, which may have accounted for half of the inflationary increase.[51] A $35,000 investment in the S&P 500 at the beginning of

---

[50]I excluded from my rental income $6,405 that was generated during the days around the Super Bowl, which took place in February 2023 at State Farm Stadium in Glendale, Arizona. Like other hosts in the area, I charged a premium for those days. The total profit on the property was $48,792 in 2023. I excluded that premium income because I didn't want it to overstate profits for future yearly projections.

[51]Sarah Gonzalez, "Economists Are Reconsidering how much Corporate Profits Drive Inflation," National Public Radio ("All Things Considered," May 19, 2023), retrieved December 23, 2023 from https://www.npr.org/2023/05/19/1177180972/economists-are-reconsidering-how-much-corporate-profits-drive-inflation>. Andrew Glover, José Mustre-del-Río, and Alice von Ende-Becker, "How Much Have Record Corporate Profits

2023 would now generate a profit of $8,750 at the end of the year ($35,000 × 25%).

That's incredible.

But it still was nearly less than one-fifth of what my property generated — and I even used a conservative 5 percent annualized gain to calculate the appreciation (see Appendix 1, column C).[52] My estimated total return on investment (ROI) for the year was 121 percent ($42,387 ÷ $35,000), nearly five times higher than the 25 percent stock gain. Even if I exclude appreciation, my property still produced a profit twice as high ($19,387) and an ROI of 55 percent.

Now, if a short-term rental property can demolish a 25 percent return in the stock market, what could that property do against a normal rate of return in the stock market (7.5%) over a longer (10-year) period of time?

These mind-blowing results are presented in Figure 4.1 on the next page.

During the first year, a $35,000 investment in the S&P 500 would generate a profit of $2,625 using the average annualized gain of 7.5 percent ($35,000 × 7.5%). Over a 10-year period, the stocks would return a profit of $37,138, which is an ROI of 106 percent ($37,138 ÷ $35,000).[53] In other words, the investment doubled in value.

Impressive.

But my rental home would do better — *much better.*

Contributed to Recent Inflation?" *Economic Review*, Federal Reserve Bank of Kansas City (First Quarter, 2023), retrieved 12/23/23 from <https://www.kansascityfed.org/documents/9329/EconomicReviewV108N1GloverMustredelRiovonEndeBecker.pdf>.

[52]An appraisal in December 2022 put the value of my property at $460,000. From 2023 to 2024, the value of my home increased 17 percent, according to the Maricopa County Assessor's office (see <https://mcassessor.maricopa.gov/mcs/?q=20739388&mod=pd>). But to make the projections in Figure 2.1, I used a much more conservative 5 percent annualized gain, which is even slightly lower than the national average of 5.9 percent for the past 52 years.

[53]Return on investment (ROI) measures the amount of return on an investment relative to the investment's cost. See footnote 30 for details.

Figure 4.1

Profits from Stocks vs. My Short-Term Rental Home

My first-year gain of $42,387 would be 16 times greater than the stock market's. My annualized gain the first year would be 121 percent, compared to just 7.5 percent for the stock market. At the end of 10 years, I would have a $572,843 profit, compared to $37,138 for the stock investor.

Phenomenal.

But how can my property generate profits much faster than stocks when stocks have a higher annualized gain?

The answer, as I've noted before, is that the gain from appreciation is calculated on the entire value of the home, not just the $35,000 that I invested.

I leveraged *other people's money* (OPM) to make money.

A stock investor can't do that.

How Leveraging Other People's Money Works

The principle behind leveraging other people's money to invest in rental real estate is simple:

Put as little down on a mortgage loan as you can, because as your property increases in value (and in the long term it always does), you get all of that appreciated value, not just the appreciation on the money you put down.

If you pay full price for your property, you still get all of the appreciated value, but the problem is that all of your money is stuck in one house. A *trapped asset*, I call it.[54]

In contrast, when you put the minimum down, you get the biggest bang for the buck in terms of your return on investment. Your profit will be higher in relation to your cost of investment. In addition, putting as little down as possible means you can use the remainder of your assets to invest in other projects. That's one of the reasons why real estate investors get wealthy so quickly.

But what if the value of the property drops?

You lose money — *but only if you sell.*

If you wait long enough, property values will come back. That has always been true in modern history.

The best example of this occurred in 2008, when housing values plummeted after lending institutions pressured Fannie Mae to ease lending standards[55] and then engaged in fraudulent and predatory lending

---

[54]Of course, you can tap that asset through a home equity loan or a cash out refinance loan, but mortgaging the purchase likely would have given you a lower interest rate.

[55]Steven A. Holmes, "Fannie Mae Eases Credit to Aid Mortgage Lending," *The New York Times* (September 30, 1999), retrieved 7/25/23 from <https://www.nytimes.com/1999/09/30/business/fannie-mae-eases-credit-to-aid-mortgage-lending.html>. This article

practices.[56] What is particularly disturbing about the housing crisis (often called the "Great Recession") is that not one financial official was ever held criminally responsible. Politicians and government prosecutors were afraid to punish the lawbreakers,[57] partly because the financial sector of the economy contributes more money to federal election campaigns and political parties than any other single source.[58]

But downturns in housing values are a very rare event. In fact, since 1950, only once has the housing real estate market declined by more than 20 percent, and that was in 2008, during the Great Recession.[59] In contrast, as I've noted earlier, the stock market has had more than a dozen 20 percent-plus declines since World War II.[60]

The long-term history of housing values in America is the history of increasing values. Properties appreciate in part because there is and always has been a shortage of housing in America. Properties generally appreciate faster than the inflation rate, which is usually about 3 percent per year. That means real estate investors profit from appreciation.

Still skeptical about the value of leveraging other people's money?

---

was fact checked by Snopes. See David Mikkelson, "Fact Check: Fannie Mae Eases Credit to Aid Mortgage Lending," Snopes (October 2, 2008), retrieved 7/25/23 from <https://www.snopes.com/fact-check/credit-canard>.

[56]Erin Coghlan, Lisa McCorkell, and Sara Hinkley, "What Really Caused the Great Recession?" Institute for Research on Labor and Employment (September 19, 2018), retrieved 7/17/23 from <https://irle.berkeley.edu/publications/irle-policy-brief/what-really-caused-the-great-recession>.

[57]Marketplace.org, "You Asked, We Answered: Why Didn't Any Wall Street CEOs Go to Jail after the Financial Crisis? It's Complicated," retrieved 7/20/23 from <https://features.marketplace.org/why-no-ceo-went-jail-after-financial-crisis>.

[58]The financial sector includes insurance companies, securities and investment firms, real estate interests, and commercial banks. See "Open Secrets, Summary of Statistics on Donations to Political Campaigns, 1990–2022" (undated), retrieved 7/20/23 from <https://www.opensecrets.org/industries/indus.php?Ind=F>.

[59]U.S. Census Bureau and U.S. Department of Housing and Urban Development, "Median Sales Price of Houses Sold for the United States [MSPUS]" (August 11, 2023), retrieved 8/12/23 from <https://fred.stlouisfed.org/series/MSPUS>.

[60]Mark Fonville, "Understanding Stock Market Corrections and Crashes," Covenant Wealth Advisors (2022), retrieved 7/25/23 from <www.covenantwealthadvisors.com/post/understanding-stock-market-corrections-and-crashes>.

Let me show you in hard numbers how much money you can make when you leverage other people's money.

It's shocking (*in a good way*).

The Phenomenal Power of Leverage

To illustrate the power of leverage, I will compare four hypothetical investors: two stock market and two real estate.

One stock market investor and one real estate investor each invest $75,000, with the latter using the money as a 25 percent down payment on a $300,000 rental home. The remaining $225,000 is mortgaged. The other two investors each invest $300,000 — one puts everything into the S&P fund and the other purchases a $300,000 rental home outright.

This analysis assumes that each of the investors is single and works another job that pays between $44,726 and $95,375. Most new real estate investors usually work another job and will need a source of earned income to qualify for a loan to purchase a rental property. This assumption also makes it easier to show how depreciation and *capital gains* taxes are calculated.[61] If your income is low, these tax benefits can be carried over and deducted later when your income is higher.

With an income between $45K and $95K, profits in 2023 from rental income are subject to a 22 percent federal earned income tax rate[62] and stock investment profits are subject to a long-term capital gains tax of 15 percent.[63] Long term means one year or more. So if you buy and sell your stocks after one year, you get the 15 percent rate on your profits. If

---

[61]The long-term capital gains tax rate in 2023 for incomes below $44,625 is zero, while earned income is taxed at 10% and 12%, depending on income.

[62]Sabrina Parys and Tina Orem, "2022-2023 Tax Brackets and Federal Income Tax Rates," Nerdwallet (Aug. 2, 2023), retrieved 8/12/23 from <https://www.nerdwallet.com/article/taxes/federal-income-tax-brackets>.

[63]Nadia Ahmad, "2023 Capital Gains Tax Rates," SmartAsset (April 21, 2023), retrieved 8/12/23 from <https://smartasset.com/taxes/2021-capital-gains-tax-rates>.

you sell in less than a year, you are taxed at the 22 percent rate.

This is one of the reasons why rich people get richer faster than poorer people. Much of their money is invested and is taxed at a lower rate than people who earn all of their income through their jobs. By the way, real estate investors also benefit from lower capital gains tax rates when they sell their properties (see discussion later in this chapter).

Each of these four investors is represented in the columns at the top of Table 4.1 on the following page. Row A shows the immediate taxable sources of income. Per my previous discussion about average annualized gains, the stock investors' funds generate a return of 7.5 percent. So the gain or profit after one year is $5,625 for the $75,000 investment and $22,500 for the $300,000 investment.

The short-term rental income for the two property investors is $52,800. This figure is based on an estimated gross rental income of $4,400 a month and is taken from Appendix 2 (column D, right side). The amount is slightly lower than the 2023 income reported on my property (see Appendix 1, column D) and is about twice as much as national average long-term rental property rates for homes of that value (also presented in Appendix 2, column D, left side). Some real estate investors contend that short-term rentals earn three to five times as much as a long-term rental, but that has not been my experience. I prefer to use more conservative estimates for this illustration.

The rental investments also draw tax-deferred gains from appreciation, which is estimated at 5 percent per year (slightly less than the 52-year average of 5.9%). So the appreciation is estimated at $15,000 ($300,000 × 5%; see row B). (The appreciation becomes a capital gain when the property is sold and, for these investors, would be taxed at 15 percent.)

The mortgaged property also draws $2,286 in principal from mortgage payments (see Appendix 2, column E, which are based on a 7 percent fixed interest loan of $225,000, see column G).

Table 4.1

The Effect of Leverage on Profits and Taxes

Estimates based on Earned Income with a 22% tax rate, single filer ($44,725 to $95,375)

	S&P 500 Stock Investors		Short-Term Rental Property Investors $300,000 Home	
One Year Returns	$75,000 Invested	$300,000 Invested	Mortgage $75,000 Down	Paid cash $300,000 Invested
A. Taxable Sources of Income				
Stock Gain (7.5%)	$5,625	$22,500	$0	$0
Rent Income ($4,400 per mo.)	$0	$0	$52,800	$52,800
B. Tax-Deferred Income Sources				
Appreciation (5% gain)	$0	$0	$15,000	$15,000
Equity from Principal	$0	$0	$2,286	$0
C. Total Taxable and Tax-Deferred				
Sources of Income (A + B)	$5,625	$22,500	$70,086	$67,800
D. Total Expenses (see Appendix 2)	$0	$0	$29,763	$11,800
E. Taxable Income Before				
Depreciation (A – D)	NA	NA	$23,037	$41,000
F. Tax Bill Before Depreciation (22%)	NA	NA	$5,068	$9,020
G. Taxable Income After $8,727				
Depreciation Deduction	NA	NA	$14,310	$32,273
H. Tax Bill (TB)	$844	$3,375	$3,148	$7,100
I. TB as % of Profits (H ÷ [C – D])	15%	15%	8%	13%
J. Profit after Taxes (Taxable &				
Non-Taxable Income; C – D – H)	$4,387	$19,125	$37,175	$48,900
K. Funds available for investing	$0	$0	$225,000	$0
L. Income from $225,000 invested	$0	$0	$111,525	$0
M. First-Year Profit after all				
funds are invested (J + L)	$4,387	$19,125	**$148,700**	$48,900

Table adapted from Appendix 2.

The total taxable and tax-deferred sources of income for each of the four investors are shown in row C of Table 4.1. The rental property investors' incomes are much higher, of course, because their investments generate revenue from rent and appreciation. But expenses (row D) must be deducted, which reduces the profits for the mortgage investor to $23,037 and $41,000 for the cash buyer. The cash buyer's expenses are much lower because there is no mortgage payment (see Appendix 2, column G).

The two property investors would have to pay $5,068 and $9,020 in federal taxes, respectively, if they couldn't depreciate the property (see row F). But each gets to deduct $8,727 in depreciation, so that reduces their tax bills to $3,148 and $7,100 (see row H).

The tax bill for the cash real estate buyer is twice as high as the bill for the $300,000 stock investor. But the cash buyer's profit is more than twice as high, $48,900 v. $19,125 (see row J). And the mortgage investor's profit is eight times greater than the profit posted by the $75K S&P investor ($37,175 v. $4,387, see row J).

Although the mortgage investor's profits are lower than the cash buyer's profits ($37,175 v. $48,900), the mortgage investor has $225,000 left over to invest in other projects. If the mortgage investor purchased three more properties of the same value and rented them, that investor would generate $111,525 more in profits ($37,175 × 3).

So, in theory, the mortgage investor would generate profits that are three times greater than the cash buyer and seven times greater than the $300K S&P investor.[64]

The results are summarized in Figure 4.2.

The bottom line is that leverage is key to growing wealth quickly.

---

[64]These results are theoretical. In the real world, an investor who had $300,000 in cash might need a large income to obtain mortgages for four other $300,000 properties. But my purpose here is to show that leverage is the key to growing wealth.

Figure 4.2

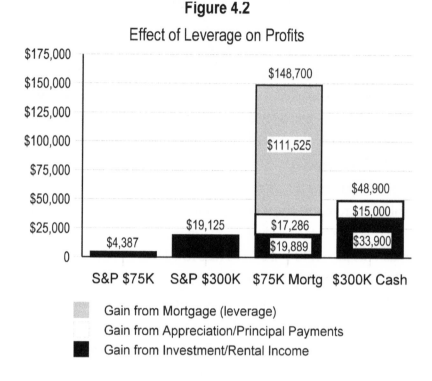

Effect of Leverage on Profits

Gain from Mortgage (leverage)
Gain from Appreciation/Principal Payments
Gain from Investment/Rental Income

The Lower the Down Payment, the Greater the ROI

The effect of leverage on return on investment is greater as the down payment on a mortgage decreases. Appendix 3 shows the impact with a 3.5 percent down payment on a $300,000 rental home ($14,000). This down payment amount is typical on an FHA loan.

The return on investment over 10 years for a 3.5 percent down payment is a whopping 3,507 percent (see Appendix 3, Column B, bottom of page), compared to 708 percent for a 25 percent down payment on an identical home (see Appendix 2, Column B, bottom of page, and only 106 percent when that $14,000 is invested into the stock market (see Column A, bottom box, Appendix 2 or 3).

Table 4.2
Capital Gains Tax Brackets for 2023

FILING STATUS	0% RATE	15% RATE	20% RATE
Single	Up to $44,625	$44,626 – $492,300	Over $492,300
Married filing jointly	Up to $89,250	$89,251 – $553,850	Over $553,850
Married filing separately	Up to $44,625	$44,626 – $276,900	Over $276,900
Head of household	Up to $59,750	$59,751 – $523,050	Over $523,050

More Reasons Why Real Estate Is So Profitable

As noted above, the single most important factor explaining why real estate is more profitable than stocks and other investments is appreciation through leverage. But there are several more.

1. Appreciation Through Leverage

Mortgaging a property allows you to leverage other people's money to maximize gains in appreciation. Rental real estate also offers a lot of tax advantages. Following is a brief discussion on three other financial advantages, some of which will be addressed in more depth later.

2. Capital Gains Tax Advantage

Like earned income, rental income is taxed at ordinary income tax rates, which vary from 10 to 37 percent, depending upon income and filing status. (The top bracket increases to 39.6% in 2025.) But Table 4.2 show that profits from the sale of a property held for more than a year are taxed at capital gains rates, which are 0, 15, and 20 percent. There is zero tax when your combined capital gain and earned income is less than $44,625. You will pay 15 percent when your combined income is between $44,626 and $492,300 and only 20 percent above that amount.[65]

One of the big advantages of capital gains income is that it isn't subject to FICA taxes, which includes Social Security, Medicare, and Medicaid taxes. That saves about 15 percent off your tax bill.

For example, if you're single and earn $20,000 from your outside job and have a capital gain of $24,625 on a property you sold, you pay zero taxes on the capital gain. But you will have to pay FICA and federal income taxes on the $20,000 from a job, which is about $2,180.[66]

If the income from your job is $40,000 instead of $20,000, your total combined income now is $64,625, so you will pay a 15 percent capital gain tax on $20,000 (the amount above $44,625), which produces a tax bill of $3,000. The payroll and federal taxes on your $40,000 income will be $4,580. Thus, your total tax bill will be $7,580.

In contrast, if all of your income came from a job, you would pay $9,525 in federal and payroll taxes — nearly $2,000 more.

The lower tax rate on capital gains is one of the reasons why real estate investors as well as people who have passive income from stocks and other investments (also taxed at the capital gains rate) tend to accumulate wealth faster than people who earn most of their income from a job. Some people argue this is unfair, because it gives the wealthy an advantage over the poor, who don't have the disposable income to invest in stocks and real estate. But this is a debate for another time. Your goal is to maximize your income as a real estate investor.

One final comment. Real estate investors often grouse about having to pay capital gains taxes. But they should be giving thanks, because they pay much less than hourly and salaried workers.

---

[65]High income earners ($200,000+ for unmarried and $250,000+ for married) also have to pay a 3.8 percent Net Investment Income Tax.

[66]To calculate these numbers, I used the 2023 capital gains calculator at Nerdwallet <https://www.nerdwallet.com/article/taxes/capital-gains-tax-rates>.

3. Hedge Against Inflation

Rental properties are a better hedge against inflation than the stock market and other investments because (1) property almost always appreciates in value faster than the inflation rate, (2) with a mortgage you get appreciation not just on the down payment but on the mortgaged amount, and (3) rental rates tend to climb faster than inflation.

I've already pointed out that the annualized rate of appreciation for homes is 5.9 percent. This is higher than the inflation rate, which has averaged about 3 percent per year since 1984.[67] Over the same time period, median personal income only increased an average of about 3.6 percent per year.[68]

Since 1980, monthly apartment asking rental rates have increased at an annualized rate of 4.9 percent, going from $308 to $1,874.[69] The rates have increased even more recently. The bottom line is that your rental property is a better hedge against inflation than your income or stocks.[70]

4. Tax-Free Equity Income

Have you ever wondered how wealthy real estate entrepreneurs often make millions from their properties but pay no taxes?

---

[67]CPI Inflation Calculator, available at Official Data.org (no date), retrieved 12/26/23 from <https://www.officialdata.org/1984-dollars-in-2022?amount=0.65>.

[68]"Median Personal Income in the United States, 1984 to 2022," U.S. Census Bureau (2022), retrieved December 26, 2023 from <https://alfred.stlouisfed.org/series?seid= MEPAINUSA646N>.

[69]"Monthly Median Asking Rent for Unfurnished Apartments in the United States from 1980 to 2023," Statista.com (undated), retrieved December 26, 2023 from <https://www.statista.com/statistics/200223/median-apartment-rent-in-the-us-since-1980>.

[70]Some economists argue that stock prices are a hedge against inflation, because inflation costs are built into the increased prices for their goods and services. See Jeremy Siegel, "Stocks Can Be Your Best Hedge Against Inflation," *Washington Post*, retrieved 9/25/19 from <https://www.washingtonpost.com/business/stocks-can-be-your-best-hedge-against-inflation/ 2011/05/17/ AFj9tc8G_story.html>.

One of their strategies is to draw their compensation not from the rental income on their properties but from the equity in their properties. They pay no taxes on equity income and it's perfectly legal.

It works like this.

You buy a property, and after 5 to 8 years or so, when equity in the property has built up, you refinance the property and take out extra cash to compensate yourself. That cash isn't income. It's equity, and equity isn't taxed.

Here's an example.

You purchase a rental property for $400,000 and put 25 percent down ($100,000). You owe the lender $300,000. One-fourth of your property is equity, but you can't draw on it because that's the cushion for the lending institution.

So you let a few years pass.

At an annualized appreciation rate of 6 percent, your property would be worth $535,000 in five years. You owe the bank about $285,000 on the original loan ($15,000 went toward principal).

The equity in the property is now $250,000 ($535,000 – $285,000). The lender will loan you 50 to 75 percent of the value of the property, reserving 25 percent ($135,000) as a cushion.

Now you can borrow up to $400,000 — $285,000 of which will be used to replace the original loan and the rest (up to $115,000) goes into your pocket. You can use that money to put a down payment on another rental property or you can spend it. It's tax-free.

Meanwhile, you use the rental income generated by your rental property to pay all the bills, including the mortgage. You don't pay yourself from the rental income, because it's taxable. Instead, you spend it on improving the property, buying another property, or paying off expenses. The goal is to spend about the same amount as you earn in rental income. That way your income on the property is close to zero and you pay no federal taxes. But you have $115,000 tax-free cash in your pocket.

Some people argue this is unfair, maybe even immoral.

But it's legal.

One final comment.

As a practical matter, refinancing a property to draw income works best with higher-priced properties, because there are closing costs associated with obtaining a new mortgage. Big time real estate investors with large apartment complexes draw millions from equity to pay themselves. Some day you may join them.

What about Depreciation, Interest, Asset Protection?

Depreciation, the mortgage interest deduction, and asset protection are sometimes identified as advantages of investing in real estate, but are they? Depends.

Depreciation

As I mentioned in Chapter 2, every year you get to depreciate a rental property 3.64 percent of the value of the property (not the land). This can save you several thousands of dollars in taxes if you have a significant amount of income to write off (typically $46,000 in earned income or more).

But when you sell the property, the IRS requires you to pay a depreciation recapture tax, which is 25 percent of the amount you wrote off. So, if you depreciated $40,000 over a 10-year period, you will owe about $10,000 in taxes.

Ouch.

Some of that sting is taken out by the fact that you are paying back the recapture tax in cheaper dollars. Getting a tax break in the early years of your business may also help you get your business on solid ground.

But depreciation might be better thought of as "a wash."

With a couple of exceptions.

If you sell your property and purchase one of equal value or higher, the recapture tax on the property you sold is wiped out and starts fresh with the new property. So that can save you a substantial amount. Capital gains taxes are also deferred.

Reinvesting profits to eliminate the recapture tax and to "defer recognition of capital gains" is known as a *1031 Exchange* (the name comes from Section 1031 of the United States Internal Revenue Code).

There are at least two other ways to avoid paying the recapture tax and capital gains taxes. You can bequeath your property to friends or loved ones, or you can sell your property at a price lower than the depreciated value (not normally a good option, of course).

Mortgage Interest Deduction

The mortgage interest deduction is often thought of as a big benefit of investing in real estate. But it's simply a business expense. Anything you spend to run a business is deductible, so it's no different than any other expense.

The attention the interest deduction continues to draw may stem in part from the fact that most homeowners no longer qualify to deduct the interest payments on their mortgage because the standard deductions were doubled a couple of years ago. Only about 10 percent are able to take this deduction.

Asset Protection

When you invest in stocks, you have no protection if the value drops or the company goes out of business. You lose your investment.

But real estate rarely drops to zero, even in tough times, like the 2008 recession. The average decline at the lowest point in 2011 was 20 percent. Some areas were hit harder, but real estate never goes to zero because the improvements on the property still have value.

But there is a downside to owning property. It increases your liability exposure. If someone is injured on your property and wins a settlement that is larger than your insurance coverage, you are out of luck.

Having an adequate insurance policy is important, of course. But the ability to insure your property doesn't necessarily give you an advantage over stocks, because they are not subject to burning down or to lawsuits (unless you are engaging in illegal activity).

Another way to protect your personal assets is to create a limited liability company (LLC). If your business is sued, your other personal assets, like your house, bank accounts, and investments, are protected because they aren't part of your LLC. Most landlords create separate LLCs for each property, because if one of your tenants falls in the shower and is injured, all of the properties under your LLC would be liable for damages. I'll show you how to create an LLC in Chapter 10.

Part II

How to Tap Your Assets

Your Job as an Asset

Thus far I've shown you how I made money in real estate, why real estate crushes the stock market, and how to estimate profits on a typical rental property.

You probably agree with me that rental real estate is far superior to the stock market when it comes to return on investment. But, you may be thinking, "Dr. Dave had an advantage as an investor because he owned his $460,000 rental home mortgage-free, so it was easy for him to tap his assets and buy another rental. But I don't own any property and don't have a lot of cash to invest. What am I to do?"

Point taken.

In the rest of this chapter, I'll talk about the ways you can tap your income to obtain a mortgage. If you have never owned a home or rental home, you may have an advantage over others who have already obtained a loan through a government-backed program. All you need is enough income to cover the costs of the mortgage payments and a moderately good credit rating.

In Chapter 6, I'll show those of you who already own a home how you can tap the equity in that home to purchase a rental property. In Chapter 7, I'll show you how you can raise cash by tapping your other assets, such as your automobiles, boats, motorcycles, jewelry, tools, vacation homes, and other valuables. These assets can be sold, rented, or used as collateral to secure a loan.

And if all of these assets fail to provide you with enough money to buy a rental property, I'll show you in Part III of this book (Chapters 8 and 9) how you can tap *other people's money* (OPM) through secured or unsecured loans or by giving friends and family or investors an equity stake in your venture as partners or stockholders.

First, though, let's look at your job as an asset.

Your Job Can Get You a Mortgage

Your job, if you have one, is an *asset*.

It's something of value because it generates income for you.

If the income you make is greater than the amount you spend, then your job generates a positive cash flow. You may spend that cash, put it into a savings account, invest it in the stock market, or use it to obtain a mortgage to buy a property.

To obtain a conventional mortgage to purchase a $300,000 property, you generally would need at least 15 percent down ($45,000), or sometimes up to 25 percent ($75,000).[71] That's a lot of money, and many would-be real estate investors don't have that kind of cash lying around.

But all is not lost.

If your income is low to moderate, you likely can qualify for a low down-payment loan through one of these government programs: Federal Housing Administration (FHA), Veterans Affairs (VA), United States Department of Agriculture (USDA), Housing Finance Agency (or Authority, HFA), Fannie Mae, or Freddie Mac. These programs also

---

[71]Rene Bermudez, "How Much Is the Down Payment for a Rental Property?" Lending Tree (Nov. 3, 2023), retrieved 11/11/23 from <https://www.lendingtree.com/home/mortgage/down-payment-for-rental-property>.

offer competitive interest rates and sometimes assistance for closing costs and down payments.

The downside (*and there's always one with every deal*) is that government-backed loans (except VA) typically require buyers to purchase mortgage insurance to cover losses should you default on the loan. Those insurance payments can be substantial, adding several hundred dollars to a monthly payment. But in most cases, the payments are discontinued when the equity in the property reaches 20 percent or more. That's the point where there's enough equity to cover lender losses should you default on the mortgage.

Although you'll have to pay mortgage insurance until you reach 20 percent, more likely than not you'll make those costs up as your property appreciates in value.

Types of Government-Backed Mortgages

Listed below are some of the popular government-backed mortgage loans, most of which offer lower down payments and lower interest rates to qualifying borrowers.

FHA Loans

FHA loans are geared mostly for buyers who have limited funds for a down payment and lower credit scores.[72] Your income will have to be high enough to cover the mortgage and other living expenses, but there's

---

[72]For more information about FHA loans, see "A Beginner's Guide to FHA Loans," Chase Bank, retrieved 11/11/23 from <https://www.chase.com/personal/mortgage/education/financing-a-home/guide-to-fha-loans>, or Troy Segal, "Federal Housing Administration (FHA) Loan: Requirements, Limits, How to Qualify," Investopedia (September 29, 2023), retrieved 11/11/23, from <https://www.investopedia.com/terms/f/fhaloan.asp>.

no maximum income rule. Anyone can qualify, even if they have already had an FHA loan on previous property. In general, though, you can only have one FHA loan at a time.

The minimum down payment is only 3.5 percent if your FICO credit score is greater than 580.[73] You'll need to put down 10 percent if your score falls into the 500 to 579 range.

As of this writing, the FHA maximum loan limit is about $475,000 in low-cost areas and $1 million in more expensive areas. You must live in your home for at least one year before leasing it. There are substantial penalties for violating this rule.

To qualify for a loan, your mortgage payment, HOA fees (if any), property taxes, homeowners insurance, and mortgage insurance should be less than 31 percent of your gross income, and your mortgage payment and consumer debts should be less than 43 percent.

VA Loans

VA loans are available to most veterans and there is no down payment. To qualify, you must meet one of these four conditions in terms of your military service: (1) 181 days during peacetime, (2) 90 consecutive days during wartime, (3) more than six years with the National Guard or 90 days in the Reserves, or (4) be a spouse of service members who lost their lives in the line of duty or as a result of service-related disability. If you are no longer serving in the military, an honorable discharge also is necessary.[74]

---

[73]Lenders use the FICO credit score (Fair Isaac Corporation) to assess whether to approve loans for borrowers. The scores include information on a borrower's payment history and indebtedness. See Adam Hayes, "FICO Score," Investopedia (Feb. 18, 2023), retrieved 11/15/23 from <https://www.investopedia.com/terms/f/ficoscore.asp>.

[74]"Eligibility Requirements for VA Home Loan Programs," U.S. Department of Veterans Affairs (no date), retrieved 11/12/23 from <https://www.va.gov/housing-assistance/home-loans/eligibility>.

VA offers several types of loans that are funded by private lending institutions that participate in the program.[75] To qualify, you don't need perfect credit.

VA loans typically offer lower interest rates than conventional loans and have more lenient borrowing requirements and, of course, no down payment at closing. VA loans also never have monthly mortgage insurance, which can save you a lot of money.

VA loans may be used to purchase condominiums and manufactured homes, but not all VA private lenders will finance these property types. VA loans require you occupy your property within 60 days of purchase. You can't obtain a VA loan to purchase a vacation or investment property, but you can use it to buy a two-to-four multi-family home if you live in one of the units. You can rent your VA-mortgaged home after living in it for one year.

The VA doesn't require a minimum credit score to qualify for one of its loans, but lenders usually have minimums. Many require a minimum score of 580. As with FHA loans, lenders have minimum debt-to-income ratio requirements. They want to ensure that you don't default on the loan. Unlike FHA loans, VA loans don't have limits on what you can borrow, but lenders often set maximum amounts similar to those for conventional loans.

Although the VA doesn't require a down payment, your lender may have rules and may require you to have a higher credit score if you are putting less than 10 percent down. VA loans require borrowers to pay a funding fee, which typically ranges from 1.25 to 3.3 percent of your loan amount. That fee helps reimburse taxpayers, who ultimately are backing the loans.

------

[75]Victoria Araj, "VA Loans: Rates, Eligibility Requirements and More," Rocket Mortgage (Nov. 06, 2023), retrieved 11/12/23 from <https://www.rocketmortgage.com/learn/va-loans>.

USDA Loans

USDA (United States Department of Agriculture) loans offer no-down-payment mortgages to low-and moderate-income homebuyers in mostly designated rural areas. They also are called *rural development* or *RD loans*. Buyers with a low to moderate income can qualify.

USDA guaranteed loans allow approved lenders to provide 30-year-fixed-rate loans. If you default on the mortgage, the mortgage lender will be reimbursed up to 90 percent of the loan value. To qualify, your income should not exceed 115 percent of your *area's median income* (AMI).[76]

USDA direct loans offer low-interest loans, some as low as 1 percent to individuals with very low or low income. There is a limit on how much you can borrow. Direct loans have a fixed interest rate, which can be reduced to 1 percent if you qualify for payment assistance. The loan terms can be extended to 38 years in some cases, which reduces the size of the monthly payment.

The USDA doesn't impose a minimum credit score requirement, but USDA-approved lenders usually look for a score of at least 640. This is more stringent than the scores required for FHA and VA loans. You must live in the home for at least one year before you can rent it out.

HFA Loans

HFA loans (not to be confused with FHA loans) are offered through state agencies, often called Housing Finance Agency or Housing Finance Authority. They provide advice and sometimes financial assistance to

---

[76]Follow the link below to find the AMI in the area or neighborhood in which you are buying a house (scroll to the bottom of page): <https://singlefamily.fanniemae.com/originating-underwriting/mortgage-products/homeready-mortgage?cmpid=marqhomeready0915>.

homebuyers.[77]

Qualified buyers may obtain a 3-percent-down mortgage and down payment assistance. You don't have to be a first-time homebuyer, but you need a low-to-moderate income for the area where your home is located.

HFA loan programs partner with Fannie Mae and Freddie Mac (see discussion below), agencies that regulate the sale and purchase of many U.S. mortgages. The goal of HFA loans is to make home-buying more affordable. They can offer lower closing costs and lower monthly payments than conventional mortgages. The mortgage insurance payments also can be canceled after a few years, unlike FHA loans.

Freddie restricts HFA loans to the purchase of single-family houses. Fannie allows applicants to buy 2- to 4-unit homes, but you have to live in one of the units. Fannie allows limited cash-out refinancing while Freddie doesn't. To qualify, you must have a minimum credit score of 620.

Fannie Mae and Freddie Mac Loans

Fannie Mae and Freddie Mac buy loans from lenders and then package them for resale in the investment marketplace.[78] Each also offers loan programs through private mortgage lenders to assist low and moderate income consumers.

---

[77]Peter Warden, "Guide to HFA Loans: What Is an HFA Loan and Who Qualifies?" The Mortgage Reports (April 19, 2022), retrieved November 11, 2023 from <https://themortgagereports.com/75528/hfa-loan-guide-preferred-and-advantage>.

[78]The difference between Fannie Mae and Freddie Mac is that the former tends to buy loans from larger commercial banks and lenders and the latter usually buys loans from smaller banks or credit unions. For more information about their programs, see Victoria Araj, "Fannie Mae vs Freddie Mac: What's The Difference?" Rocket Mortgage (October 27, 2023), retrieved 11/9/23 from <https://www.rocketmortgage.com/learn/fannie-mae-vs-freddie-mac>.

Fannie Mae offers a program called HomeReady and Freddie Mac offers Home Possible,[79] which help those who are unable to come up with a standard 20-percent down payment. The main difference is that your credit score for a Home Possible loan must be at least 660 and for a HomeReady loan at least 620.

A HomeReady mortgage only requires borrowers to put down 3 to 5 percent. Unlike conventional mortgages, a HomeReady mortgage allows you to accept gifts from friends and family toward your down payment. You also are allowed to cancel your mortgage insurance once you've paid down 20 percent of your home's value.

A HomeReady loan also can be used to refinance your current home loan to lower your monthly payment, but you can't draw any cash from your equity.

Requirements to Qualify for a Mortgage

The requirements to qualify for a mortgage vary from program to program and lender to lender. Here are four major elements that most loan program take into account when deciding to issue a mortgage.

- *Debt-to-Income Ratio Requirements.* The DTI ratio is a measure of your income against your debts. To calculate, divide your monthly debt payments by your gross monthly income. Although there is no minimum income requirement, the ratio typically ranges between 36 percent and 43 percent, depending on the type of loan, your credit rating, and the amount of the down payment.

- *Sources of Income that Qualify for a Mortgage.* Your gross monthly

---

[79]Victoria Araj, "HomeReady Mortgage: Do You Qualify For This Loan?" Rocket Mortgage (June 22, 2023), retrieved 11/13/2023 from <https://www.rocketmortgage.com/learn/homeready>.

income can come from a number of sources, including your employment income (wages, bonuses, commissions, etc.); Schedule K-1 income from partnerships, estates and corporations; retirement income (401(k), IRA, 403(b), and pensions); rental income; disability payments; Social Security; dividend or interest income; alimony and child support; and trust income. You'll need to offer documents and evidence (such as pay stubs) to count this income.

- *Steady Employment Record.* Some lenders require two years of income from the same employer, but this can vary. Switching jobs just before getting a loan can make it more difficult to obtain a mortgage.

- *Credit Score.* Conventional loans often require a FICO score of 620. FHA allows scores as low as 580 for a 3.5 percent down payment and 500 for 10 percent down, although not all lenders will offer these rates. In addition, the higher your score, typically the lower your interest rate. VA doesn't have any set minimums but they typically are similar to FHA.

Your Home as an Asset

When it comes to raising money for a rental investment, your home may be the single-most important asset you have. As obvious as this may seem, many people overlook this, even me. Before I began writing the introductory real estate book for Ken McElroy, I never thought of leveraging the equity in my home to purchase a rental property.

But one of the advantages of borrowing on the equity in your home is that you get to continue living in it. And when you use it to buy another property, you'll have two properties generating equity through appreciation. Both of my properties are appreciating about 10 percent a year, which means I am earning about $71,000 in appreciation per year. I do have some expenses in maintaining the properties, but I get a tax write-off on that because I lease both properties (half of my condo is leased to a family member).

Equity in Your Home

If you own a home but can't qualify for a low down-payment mortgage and don't have the cash to cover a 25 percent down payment, consider tapping into the equity in your home or another property you own. Typically you'll need to have about 40 percent equity or more in your home to make this worthwhile.

When you obtain a mortgage to buy a home, you normally have very little equity in the property, especially if the mortgage is government-backed and requires only small or no down payments. Even if you put down 20 percent, this level of equity isn't high enough to qualify you for an equity loan. Most lending institutions require a minimum equity reserve of 20 percent to use as a cushion should they have to foreclose on the property. The upshot is that you'll need about 40 percent equity in your property to obtain an equity loan, and you'll only be able to draw half of that, or 20 percent of the home's value.

So if you put 20 percent down on a home, how long does it typically take before you accumulate enough equity to borrow on it?

Roughly five years.

A typical home appreciates in value about 6 percent per year, which means that in five years your home will be valued about 33 percent more. If you bought the home for $300,000, it now would be worth about $400,000, giving you $100,000 in appreciated equity.

If you put down $60,000 at the time of purchase (20% of $300,000), you would now have a total of $160,000 in equity. If your credit is good, many lending institutions will loan you about half of that, or $80,000, leaving the rest ($80,000) as their 20-percent default cushion.

Types of Equity Loans

One advantage of drawing on the equity in your home is that the interest rates are typically lower than those for a personal loan, because your home equity loan is backed with collateral. There are at least four ways to draw this equity from a lender: (1) cash-out refinance mortgage, (2) home equity loans, (3) home equity lines of credit (HELOC), and (4) no monthly payment equity loans.

Cash-out Refinance Mortgage

A cash-out refinance mortgage pays off your first mortgage and gives you extra cash depending upon on how much equity is in your home.

The new mortgage pays off your original mortgage and then the lending institution gives you the rest in cash. The interest rate on the new mortgage can be fixed or adjustable. Fixed is better during an inflationary period, of course. Adjustable rates tend to be lower, at least in the beginning of the loan, but if inflation soars and loan rates go up you could end up paying lots more interest.

The biggest downside of a cash-out refinance is closing costs, which can be as much as 2 to 5 percent on a $300,000 loan. But on the upside the extra cash you pull out of the deal isn't taxed, because it's equity, not income.[80] In addition, the interest rate on the cash-out refinance mortgage is usually lower than it is for a home equity or line of credit loan, which can save you tens of thousands of dollars over the long haul.

If you invest the cash from the cash-out refinance mortgage in a business or use it to purchase another property, the interest you pay the lending institution on that loan can be deducted as an expense on either Schedule C (Business Income) or Schedule E (Rental Income).

To illustrate, let's say you obtained $50,000 in cash from a refinance mortgage and used it as a down payment to purchase a rental property. The interest you pay on that $50,000 can be deducted from your rental income. If you used some of that money to buy office supplies, those costs also can be fully deducted in the year they are spent, just like the interest payments. If you purchase a property, you can also depreciate the

---

[80]This is one of the ways that real estate investors avoid paying taxes. They refinance their properties and pay themselves with the equity portion of the deal. See Chapter 4 for details.

property. Cash-out refinance mortgage loans typically offer the lowest interest rates, although closing costs can be substantial.

Home Equity Loans

A home equity loan does not replace the first mortgage on your home; rather, it's a second secured loan. The interest rate is usually higher than a first mortgage loan but it has lower closing costs.

Although an equity loan is often referred to as a second mortgage, its repayment term tends to be shorter, usually 10 to 20 years instead of 30. The shorter term means the monthly payment is higher but the upside is that you pay less interest over time.

It's generally easier to obtain a home equity loan from your original mortgage lender than from a new one. That's because, if there's a foreclosure on the property, the first lien is paid off before the second equity loan lien, and being in second place means there may not be enough equity left in the property to pay that lien off in full. Another advantage of the home equity loan is that it takes less time and effort to complete than a full-scale mortgage, which can take weeks or even months.

Home Equity Line of Credit

The third type of home equity loan is called a HELOC loan, and it's basically a revolving line of credit that has an adjustable interest rate. You pay interest on the amount you borrow, not on the total line of credit.

The interest rate is based on the *prime rate* plus a margin.[81]

---

[81]The prime rate is the interest rate that commercial banks charge their most creditworthy customers. The rate is based on the Federal Reserve's federal funds overnight rate. Banks usually charge about three percentage points more than what the Federal

The interest rate on a line of credit is usually higher than a home equity loan. A HELOC gives you a set amount of time to draw on your credit line, such as five years. Once you take the money, you'll begin making monthly principal and interest payments. After the draw period ends, you will continue to make payments until the outstanding balance is paid off. HELOCs often have to be paid in 20 years or less.

HELOC and traditional home equity loans are no longer tax deductible on Schedule A (personal deductions). But they can be deducted or depreciated when used for business purposes, such as for the purchase of an investment property or a refrigerator for a rental property. Like a home equity loan, HELOCs typically have lower fees than cash-out and conventional mortgage loans but higher rates than home equity loans.

No Monthly Payment Equity Loans

Does that headline sound too good to be true?

Of course, there's always a catch.

With a no monthly payment equity loan, you don't have to make monthly payments until you sell the property or a certain amount of time passes, such as 10 years.

The private equity loan company will require you to pay a closing fee of 3 percent or so and will take a large share of the equity in your home (8% to 25%) when you sell or when 10 years is up. The lender typically hires the appraiser, which is problematic for you, the borrower, as appraisers have a long history of distorting home values to favor their clients.[82]

Reserve charges them. For more information, see James Chen, "Prime Rate Definition," Investopedia (August 05, 2023), retrieved 11/15/23 from <https://www.investopedia.com/terms/p/primerate.asp> .

[82]During the 2008 housing crash, appraisers deflated or inflated the values of homes so loan deals could close. Rules were tightened but some abuse continues.

To simplify the analysis, let's assume your home is worth $100,000 and you draw $25,000 of equity on the house, which is 25 percent of the total value. In 10 years, your home will be worth $180,000 (6% interest appreciation per year). Lending companies in this field typically charge about 20 percent of that equity,[83] in addition to the $25,000 in principal that you owe. That means you will owe the lending company $36,000 in interest. Your total payback will be $61,000.

By way of comparison, had you taken out a conventional home equity loan at 6 percent interest, you would have paid about $8,300 in interest costs in addition to the principal. This would have saved you $27,700 ($36,000 – $8,300), but you would have had to make payments on the home equity loan every month for 10 years. The bottom line is that you should be cautious in choosing a no monthly payment equity loan. A lot depends upon the percentage of profit the lender takes.

Reversing Your Mortgage

If you are 62 or older, another way to raise capital is the *reverse mortgage*, which is basically an equity loan without monthly payments.

This is similar to a no monthly payment equity loan. You keep the title to your property but get to live in it until you die or permanently move out of the home. At that time, the principal and interest on the loan must be repaid to the lender. In some cases, the lender takes full ownership of your home.

You must have a lot of equity to qualify for a reverse mortgage. You also must continue to maintain your home and pay insurance and taxes.

---

[83]The companies do not publish their rates, but you can get an estimate at their websites. See "Hometap ADU Financing Review," Prefabreview.com (June 1, 2020), retrieved 10/1/20 from <https://www.prefabreview.com/ blog/hometap-adu-financing-review>. The article estimated Hometap's take was 35 percent.

The equity payments can be taken in one lump sum, as a line of credit, or in monthly installments. The lump-sum payment is the most expensive, because interest begins when the money is received. You normally can draw up to 60 percent of the total value of the home if you have that much equity.

The money you receive generally is not taxable, because it's equity, not income. One downside is that your heirs may be disappointed, because they will inherit less or nothing at all, depending upon the contract.

There are three major types of reverse mortgages:

- *The single-purpose reverse mortgage* is the least expensive option for you. They are available through state and local governments and non-profit organizations. The loan usually must be used to pay for home repairs or improvements, or property taxes. Most homeowners qualify.

- *Proprietary reverse mortgages* are loans backed by private profit-seeking companies. Usually you can use the money for any purpose, since the loan is collateralized and the lender can take ownership of the house if you fail to pay.

- *The Home Equity Conversion Mortgage* (HECM) is insured and backed by the U.S. Department of Housing and Urban Development. If there isn't enough equity in the home to repay the loan at the end of the agreement, then the federal government makes up the difference. HECM loans can be used for any purpose, and the amount available can depend on your age, type of mortgage, appraised value of your home, interest rates, your ability to pay property taxes, and homeowner's insurance.

Proprietary and HECM reverse mortgages tend to have higher interest rates than conventional home loans. Up-front costs also can be high. Normally you take one of these loans if you don't plan to stay in your home for a long time. The interest payments on a reverse mortgage are not tax deductible unless used for business purposes.

Reverse mortgages, like no monthly payment loans, are controversial, because they are complex and it's difficult for consumers to determine whether they are getting a good deal. *Consumer Reports* does not recommend them.[84] Also, if borrowers fail to pay property insurances and taxes, lenders can foreclose on their homes.

---

[84]"Don't Be Suckered into Buying a Reverse Mortgage: Advertisements Make Them Sound Tempting but Reverse Mortgages Can Put Your Retirement at Risk," *Consumer Reports* (July 15, 2015), retrieved 10/12/23 from <https://www.consumerreports.org/cro/news/ 2015/07/don-t-be-suckered-into-buying-a-reverse-mortgage/index.htm>.

Your Autos and Other Stuff as Assets

In addition to equity in your home, other assets that can be used as collateral for loans include automobiles, motorcycles, boats, and jewelry. These items also can be rented or sold.

To obtain a loan on your automobile, you'll need a substantial amount of equity in the car. Junkers don't qualify.

Your best bet is to seek a loan from a credit union, because they typically offer the lowest interest rates (they are not-for-profit organizations). Some commercial banks make collateralized auto loans, but many don't like them because they don't generate a lot of profit. Many publicly owned banks prefer to maximize profits through market investments and commercial loans. This keeps the value of their stock up, which provides substantial financial benefits to top managers and stockholders.[85]

Title loan lenders also offer collateralized auto loans, but the annual interest rates on these loans can be astronomical, often 100 percent or

---

[85]A fair amount of research suggests that public corporations respond more eagerly to the needs of their top-level managers than to those of their shareholders. See David Demers, "Who Controls the Editorial Content at Corporate News Organizations? An Empirical Test of the Managerial Revolution Hypothesis," *World Futures: The Journal of General Evolution, 57*: 2001, pp 103-123, and David Demers and Debra Merskin, "Corporate News Structure and the Managerial Revolution," *Journal of Media Economics,* 13(2): 2000, pp. 103-121.

higher.[86] Like conventional lenders, title loan lenders place a lien on the title to your car and will repossess it if you default on the loan.

It's more difficult to obtain collateralized loans on motorcycles, boats, and jewelry, because these items often are more difficult to resell than an automobile and because they often have less value than autos. Most conventional lending institutions also will not offer collateralized loans on these items, but pawn shops often do. Be cautious before entering into any consignment or loan agreement. A signed contract is a binding contract unless the pawn shop engages in fraud.

Personal Loans

Many lending institutions offer uncollateralized personal loans. The interest rates on these unsecured loans are typically higher than those for collateralized loans. Credit unions almost always offer the best interest rates.

You typically need a good credit rating to get a personal loan. If you have a lot of credit card debt, a personal loan can often reduce the interest rate on that debt. This could free up income to help you obtain a mortgage or equity loan.

Payday loans are also personal loans. Although they don't require a credit check, they do require proof that you have a job. These are usually short-term loans (two weeks or so) and the interest rates can be extremely high, often 400 percent.

People who have poor credit records — and, thus, cannot obtain loans from other places — are more likely to be customers of payday loans. But if you fail to pay one of these loans on time, the interest can

---

[86]The sales pitch may avoid telling you the annual percentage rate. They often tell people that the monthly interest rate is just 10 percent, which is actually 120 percent or more a year.

compound so quickly that, for instance, a $500 loan can easily turn into thousands of dollars of debt in a few months. I do not recommend these loans.

Savings and Certificates of Deposit

If you have money in savings accounts or *certificates of deposit,* you might want to consider using it for your venture. The rates of return on these investments are often terrible — less than 2 percent — and real estate, when properly purchased and managed, will produce phenomenally higher rates of return (mine is currently producing about 121 percent annualized).

Yet many people keep their money in savings accounts and CDs because it makes them feel more financially secure. Money invested in an account insured by the Federal Deposit Insurance Corporation is more secure, because the government guarantees your funds up to $250,000 per account. If having your money in a safe place is extremely important to you, though, I doubt you're reading this book. Entrepreneurial ventures always involve some risk but, if invested wisely, big payoffs.

Renting Your Stuff

An increasingly popular method of raising capital is to lease your car, boat, or other assets.

HyreCar, for example, allows you to rent your car to drivers who work for Uber, Lyft and DoorDash. The company says "carsharing" can generate up to $12,000 a year for you. The drivers who use your car pay HyreCar, which then pays you. There is no membership fee and the company provides you free ride-share insurance. Uber and Lyft also cover damage to your auto at no extra charge when their drivers have mishaps. HyreCar says people who lease their cars have very low risk. But you should thoroughly research the advantages and disadvantages before signing with any rental service.

Turo.com is another car-sharing company, but its role is to link you to consumers rather than professional drivers. Participation in their program is free, and you can set the price or let Turo do it. The company arranges for customers to pick up the keys and vehicle from you. You earn 65 to 85 percent of the amount paid by customers, depending upon which insurance package you select.

If you don't own a car, you can rent your parking space (popular in big cities where parking spaces are expensive), part of your driveway, or space inside of your garage. Neighbor.com links you with potential renters. The rule of thumb is that you will rent your space for about half of what a commercial company charges.

Of course, you can also post your own ads on Craigslist or other sites and can rent tools and lots of other items. However, I recommend that you consult with an insurance professional or attorney to protect yourself from liability lawsuits. You can also create a limited liability company that can protect your personal assets should your business be sued or go bankrupt (see Chapter 10).[87]

Selling Your Stuff

You bought a boat a decade ago and now it's collecting dust in the back of your garage. You can sell it through Craigslist or a dozen other online services.

Table 7.1 lists some of the services that sell these items. Some

---

[87]Also see Ken McElroy, *ABCs of Buying Rental Property* (Scottsdale, KM Press: 2020), Chapter 4, and Garrett Sutton, *Start Your Own Corporation,* 3rd ed. (Scottsdale: RDA Press, 2018).

Table 7.1

Places to Sell Your Stuff

	Products Bought/Sold	Cost to You/ Offer Price	Payment*
Amazon Marketplace	Everything	99¢ per Sale	DTC Online
ArtPal	Art	Free	DTC Online
Bonanza	Everything	% of Sale	DTC Online
Craigslist	Everything	Free	In-person
Decluttr	Phones/Tech	Offers Price	Pays You
eBay	Everything	% of Sale	DTC Online
eBid	Everything	% of Sale	DTC Online
Etsy	Arts/Crafts	% of Sale	DTC Online
Facebook Marketplace	Everything	Free	DTC Online
Gazelle	Smart Phones	Offers Price	Pays You
Instagram	Everything	Ad Charge	DTC Online
LetGo	Everything	Free	In-person
OfferUp	Everything	Free	In-person
Powells.com	Books	Offers Price	Pays You
SellBackYourBook	Books	Offers Price	Pays You
SellDVDsOnline	DVD/CD etc	Offers Price	Pays You
SellMyWeddingDress	Wedding Dress	$19.95/sale	DTC Online
Shutterstock	Photographs	Pays 15%+	Pays You
*DTC = Direct to Consumer			

specialize in selling different types of products (like books or used clothing). Some sites, like Amazon Marketplace, charge you a fee for each sale and others, like eBay, take a percentage of each sale.

Some of the services will buy directly from you ("Pays You"). Most, though, ask you to post your items for sale and then sell them directly to customers who visit their website ("DTC Online" — Direct To Consumer Online). They collect the payment, take their fee, and then turn over the rest of the proceeds to you. Other services, such as Craigslist, simply link you to local customers, who you typically meet in person to close the transaction ("In-person"). This generally works best when selling more expensive items, such as automobiles and jewelry. Buyers need to inspect the goods before paying for them.

You may not get wealthy selling stuff you no longer need, but the extra cash can help you raise money for a down payment on a rental house.

Borrowing from Your Retirement Funds

When you retire, you can start spending your retirement funds. But before then, many private- and government-funded retirement plans will offers loans to you on your investment funds.

For example, investors with 401(k) plans may borrow $50,000 or 50 percent of the total amount of money in the fund (whichever is smaller).[88] That amount may not be enough to fully fund your financial venture, but it can help pay for a down payment and can be very cost-effective compared to other methods of raising capital.

That's because there's little or no cost to you. You are borrowing from yourself, so the interest on the loan you pay goes back to you. In addition, your credit rating remains unaffected, because you aren't adding to your debt load (you're borrowing your own money).

There are some drawbacks. One is that the loan payment amounts can be hefty, because the loan usually has to be repaid in five years or less (or up to 15 years when buying a home for personal use). A $50,000

---

[88]Elizabeth O'Brien, "Here's What Happens When You Take out a Loan on Your 401(k)," *Marketwatch* (June 29, 2015), retrieved October 2, 2019 from <https://www.marketwatch.com/story/avoid- the-temptation-of-dipping-into-your-401k-2015-06-04>.

loan at 6 percent interest for five years means your monthly payment will be nearly $1,000 a month.

If you're earning about 5 percent annually on your 401(k) investments, repay the loan in five years and retire at that time, the cost of the loan is only $1,923.[89] That's an incredible deal. If you're 20 years from retirement, the cost is about $4,000, which is 8 percent but that comes out to less than 1 percent interest each year. Still a great deal.

But if you fail to repay the loan, you're penalized 10 percent and your fund will have $180,000 less in it in two decades.[90]

The bottom line is that you need to repay the loan on time. Be sure to consult with a 401(k) expert before borrowing from your fund.

Using Your Credit Cards

Some (or maybe I should say "many") investors have used their credit cards to pay for business expenses, especially when they are starting up.

But credit cards are not a good long-term financial option for any kind of business, unless the balance is paid off every month. The interest rate on most cards is 25 percent and higher. Even people with superb credit will pay 12 percent or more. In late 2022, the average American was carrying $6,000 in debt.[91] So a household with two people has about

---

[89]Bankrate.com offers an online calculator where you can calculate the cost of the loan: <https://www.bankrate.com/calculators/retirement/borrow-from-401k-calculator.aspx>.

[90]If you retire and still owe on the loan, you can continue to make payments or take the balance as a withdrawal. The latter is an attractive option if your income is low.

[91]"What is the average credit card debt in America?" Capital One (October 9, 2023), retrieved 11/24/2023 from <https://www.capitalone.com/learn-grow/money-management/average-credit-card-debt-in-america>.

$12,000 in debt. Each one is paying more than $2,500 a year in interest.[92]

If you have a lot of credit card debt, pay it off as quickly as you. If you can't, then consider applying for a lower-interest personal or equity loan. Credit unions often offer the best interest rates on personal loans.

[92]Joe Resendiz, "Average Credit Card Debt in America: June 2020," ValuePenguin.com (June 17, 2020), retrieved from <https://www.valuepenguin.com/average-credit-card-debt>.

Part III
How to Tap Other People's Assets

Family and Friends as Assets

You secured an equity loan on your car, sold your jewelry and motorcycle, and rented space in your shed but still don't have enough money to launch your venture.

Before turning to professional investors or lenders, consider approaching family and friends, because most start-up capital for small businesses comes from them.

A 2010 survey of U.S. adults found that 5 percent of them had funded someone starting a business in the past three years.[93] Of those who provided funding, 32 percent said it went to a friend or neighbor, 26 percent to a close family member, 11 percent to some other relative, and 8 percent to a work colleague.

A study of millionaires also found that during the previous five years half of them had given an average of $313,200 to family members, especially children and grandchildren.[94]

Some of the people who might invest in your venture include family,

---

[93]Donna J. Kelley, Niels Bosma, José Ernesto Amorós, "2010 Global Report," Global Entrepreneurship Monitor (2010), retrieved January 21, 2024 from <https://entreprenorskapsforum.se/wp-content/uploads/2011/02/GEM-2010-Global-Report.pdf> .

[94]Robert Frank, "Millionaires Become the 'Family Bank,'" CNBC (December 17, 2013), retrieved 11/29/23 from <https://www.cnbc.com/2013/12/17/millionaires-become-the-family-bank.html>.

friends, neighbors, friends of friends, business associates, coworkers, people in your social groups, former bosses, high school and college classmates, and professionals you know, like doctors, lawyers, and accountants. Professionals tend to have higher incomes and the disposable income to invest in private ventures. Many invest in restaurants and real estate ventures.

In sum, all you need is one wealthy relative or colleague to solve your need for capital.

But before asking for money, consider at least three things to avoid getting into legal trouble and to increase your chances of securing investment money: (1) Some investments are taxable; (2) Investors have rights; and (3) Do your homework before you ask for money.

Some Investments Are Taxable

Say you have a wealthy aunt who favors you (naturally) and wants to invest in your real estate venture.

If she loans you $30,000 but doesn't expect you to pay interest, the IRS will still expect her to pay taxes on the money she loaned.[95] Even between family members, a loan is a business transaction and interest payments are taxable. If she doesn't charge you interest, the IRS will calculate it for her and add that amount to her taxable income.[96]

To avoid paying taxes, your aunt could conceal the transaction from the IRS. That happens a lot when family members gift to each other. But

---

[95] For details, see Hannah Rounds, "Family Loans: What to Know Before You Borrow or Lend within the Clan," Credit Karma (July 23, 2022), retrieved 1/21/24 from <https://www.creditkarma.com/personal-loans/i/family-loans>.

[96] The minimum loan rate for family loans in 2023 was about 4 percent. Rates vary depending upon time period and length of repayment schedule. See Trusts & Estates Practice Group, "IRS Announces AFRs for February 2023," Greensfelder Attorneys at Law (January 26, 2023), retrieved 1/21/24 from <https://www.greensfelder.com/trusts-and-estates-blog/irs-announces-afrs-for-february-2023>.

banks monitor the transfer of large sums of money into accounts, and she could be forced to pay a penalty as well.[97]

Of course, you need to inform auntie in advance of this IRS rule. But there are ways to skirt the loan-taxation problem. Auntie can gift you up to $18,000 and neither she nor you will have to pay taxes, according to IRS rules.[98] If she gives more than that, she'll be taxed on it (only the gift giver, not the receiver, is taxed). Over her lifetime, she can only give up to about $14 million. (*I suspect this will not a problem in your family.*) If auntie gives a large gift, she'll need to file Form 709 at the end of the tax year.

Another way around the loan-taxation problem is to give auntie an equity stake in your real estate business. There's no tax for anyone and no complicated paperwork. Only when your real estate business earns a profit are you and auntie subject to taxation.

A popular and easy way to provide equity to investors is through a partnership or a limited liability company (LLC). In both cases, you can still retain control of your rental business. The LLC offers *limited liability* to them and to you, too. I'll talk more about how to create a company in Chapter 10.

Investors Have Rights

When auntie writes that check, you are obligated to use it for the purpose you gave her to get the money. If you say you're going to buy a rental property but buy a boat, you could end up behind bars and in

---

[97]By the way, when bank customers withdraw or deposit large sums of money into their accounts, the bank tracks those transactions and reports them to the IRS. Among other things, the government is looking for people who launder money.

[98]Tina Orem and Sabrina Parys, "Gift Tax: How It Works, Who Pays and Rates," Nerdwallet.com (Nov. 20, 2023), retrieved 11/30/23 from <https://www.nerdwallet.com/article/taxes/gift-tax-rate>.

deep water with auntie.

Investment laws and rules are designed to protect all investors, especially unsophisticated ones like your aunt. The job of the Securities and Exchange Commission (SEC) is to discourage entrepreneurs from taking advantage of investors, sophisticated or not. The SEC limits the ways you and others can raise capital.

If you want to create a real estate corporation and sell stock to raise capital, you would register the sale with the SEC. This allows you to sell stock to anyone, including unsophisticated investors, because the SEC monitors the process. However, creating a corporation like this is extremely expensive and time-consuming and generally not a good option for a small real estate business.

You also can obtain an exemption from SEC rules. You'll need to create accurate and truthful *disclosure documents* for prospective investors. But these documents require the assistance of a business attorney and are expensive to create.

The second exemption option, which is more popular and less expensive, is to sell stock only to *accredited investors*, which includes wealthy people, banks, insurance companies, brokers, and trust funds. Accredited investors can invest in ventures not registered with the SEC. But to qualify as an accredited investor, one must earn more than $200,000 during each of the last two years ($300,000 for a couple) or have a net worth of more than $1 million (home excluded). The criteria for businesses to qualify as an accredited investor are tougher.

The SEC prevents a non-accredited investor like your aunt from investing in many private business ventures, because there are too many shysters out there. Some critics see this as paternalistic and discriminatory. But in recent years the SEC and state governments have loosened some of the rules, giving non-accredited investors access to more high-return investments, such as crowdfunding. In Arizona, non-accredited investors can put up to $10,000 into a single venture.

Although accredited investors generally have access to higher rates of returns, if those investments fail, the investors have less legal protection than non-accredited investors. Sophisticated investors are assumed to be smart enough to know what they are getting into. The reality is that most investments that need lots of money rely on accredited investors, because the means of processing funds from a large number of small-time investors are not as cost-effective.

The upshot is that when you raise funds from people for your real estate ventures, be sure to be open and honest. Truth is always a good defense. And, when it comes to raising money for a small-time real estate venture, a much better option is a limited liability company or a partnership, which allow you to bring on equity investors.

Do Your Homework Before You Beg

You've just arrived at the birthday party for your aunt.

She's talking with one of your cousins. Look at that sparkling 4-carat diamond neckless she's wearing. But is this the time to ask her whether to invest in your real estate venture?

A lot depends on how comfortable the two of you are together.

To increase the chances of getting her assistance, you should do some homework before approaching her and other potential investors.

Create a Business Plan

One approach is to put together a brief business plan. A page or two will do. The plan is basically a statement about how you intend to reach a goal of purchasing a rental property. Table 8.1 shows some of the things you should cover. Please revise or add other items as they pertain to your project.

Table 8.1

A Guide for Creating a Business Plan to Purchase a Rental Property

Criterion	Question to Solve	Elaboration/Examples
1. Goal	What are you trying to do?	Purchase a short or long-term rental home
2. Location	Where do you want to buy your property?	A general area or specific address if you have one
3. Estimated Cost	How much cash will you need to accomplish your goal?	This would include down payment, closing costs, fix-up costs, other expenses
4. Your investment	How much are you investing into the project?	Provide a specific amount and where the funds are located
5. Mortgage amount (if applicable)	How much money will you borrow to purchase the property?	Be specific. Name the institution(s) or individual(s) where you intend to obtain the funds
6. Funds needed	How much money do you need from your investors?	Be specific: identify investors who have committed funds
7. Estimated Income	How much rental income and other sources of income do you expect each month and year?	Provide details
8. Estimated Expenses	How much in expenses do you expect a month and in a year?	Provide details
9. Estimated Profits	How much money do you expect to make in the first year after the property is rented	Provide details
10. Payout to investors	How much of the profits will be paid out to investors and how?	Provide details

The purpose of a business plan is to convince your aunt and others that you are serious about buying a rental property and that you know what you're doing. The best approach isn't to give them the plan and ask for money. Instead, give them the plan and just ask for feedback. "I'm thinking of buying a rental property. Here's a rough plan of what I'd like to do. Can you give me some constructive comments?"

This approach will make your potential investors much more comfortable, especially because it shows that you value their opinion. This helps build trust.

And, before you approach people who you believe can offer the most investment money, try to get other smaller investors on board, perhaps your parents or siblings, people who really trust you. Your aunt and other investors will take your plan far more seriously when they see other people investing in it. It shows that other people trust you and makes it easier for your aunt and others to trust you, too.[99]

And that's all you need to do right now.

Don't pressure them for money. Don't oversell the idea or brag about how much money you're going to make, even though you know from reading this book that the property is likely to do well.

Just plant the idea of investing into their heads.

If they ask whether you need some money, simply respond, "That's generous of you. But not yet. Right now I'm just trying to refine my business proposal. Your feedback would be appreciated."

Your goal here is to get them to look at your business plan. If you ask them for money, some people will feel like you are trying to pressure them and they won't even look at your plan. Distribute copies of your plan to relatives, friends, colleagues, professionals you know, and coworkers.

And be patient.

---

[99]James T. Horan Jr. has created another useful guide for creating a business. He calls it "The One Page Business Plan," retrieved Oct. 27, 2023, from <http://www.imdrt.org/mentoring/2011_Horan.pdf>.

Many won't respond, of course.

But some will, especially those who care about you.

If they volunteer that they would like to invest in your venture, then you can talk about it. But don't press them for money if they don't bring the subject up first. Stay focused on the goal of making the best possible business proposal you can. If you do that, they will see that you are serious and careful in your planning. Nothing kills a potential investment faster than an impulsive, reckless person.

If you have a good plan and people trust you, there is a good chance someone will say those magic words: "I'd like to invest a few dollars in your venture." Now you have credibility. Someone besides you believes in you and what you're doing. And this makes it much easier to enlist support from others.

So let's return to the birthday party.

When you arrive, your aunt may or may not be aware you are planning to buy a property. During your casual conversation with her, if she doesn't ask you about your business plan but says, "And what have you been up to, dear?" — give her some trivial news and then mention, "Oh, I'm planning to buy a rental property and my parents are going to invest in it."

Can you see how much easier it will be to enlist auntie's support?

When it comes to sales approaches, few things are more powerful than pointing out that someone else is buying or endorsing a product or business idea. That's why celebrities are often used to sell products.

Your aunt may never invest in your venture.

But don't toss in the towel.

No entrepreneur succeeds in everything they do. Failure is a prerequisite for success. Learn from it.

And if no one invests in your business, don't blame yourself or get angry. Not everyone has a lot of cash sitting around. Most also are too afraid and don't understand a good opportunity when they see it.

When I meet a successful real estate investor, I will often say, "Your family must be proud of you. Do they invest in your projects?"

"No, they don't," many of them say. "They have never invested in my ventures. They think I got rich because of chance."

Envy denies people opportunities to help themselves.

Ignore those people and move on.

Raising Capital from Friends and Acquaintances

The discussion above focused on raising capital from family and close friends — the people you know best and are most comfortable with. Informal business plans and conversations with them generally work well.

Your pitch to coworkers and professionals likely will differ. Your doctor likely will be less influenced by your effervescent personality than by the quality of your business plan. So focus more heavily on the financial benefits of your venture.

Don't wear blue jeans and a tank top to the meeting. Dress up. Professionals appreciate others who project an air of confidence and professionalism.

Equity Stake or Loan?

In terms of raising capital to purchase a rental property, there are two major approaches. One is to give investors an equity stake in your business. The other is to borrow money from them and then pay them interest. You can also do both.

One advantage of giving an equity stake is that you don't have to pay your investor back. In contrast, when you borrow money, you typically have to start paying your investors back right away — some principal and lot of interest. If your business fails (that is, becomes insolvent), the equity investor loses his or her investment. You also lose what you invested but don't have to pay them back if you didn't engage in fraud.

A disadvantage of giving others equity in your real estate business is that can you lose some control over your venture. If you give them half ownership, you and your partner will have to work hard to avoid disputes. But if you retain more than 50 percent, you may find it more difficult to raise investment funds. These silent investors need to trust your ability to make good decisions to invest their funds.

People who invest in a business venture often expect to walk away with an equity stake. So if auntie gives you a substantial sum of money, expect to give her some ownership. Compromise is often necessary to reach one's goals.

If you don't want to share ownership, then consider borrowing money and setting up a loan repayment schedule. Of course, the riskier the investment, the higher the interest rate you'll need to pay.

As of this writing, large real estate apartment ventures seeking funds from accredited investors were offering between 7 and 10 percent interest. Smaller real estate ventures seeking funds from non-accredited investors through crowdfunding projects (see Chapter 9) were paying 10 to 12 percent. Family and friends may be content with 6 percent, but if you pay too little, they may not reinvest when you need them for a future project. Treating your investors well is itself a good investment.

If you go the loan route, you may want to defer paying your lenders for a year or two until you get established. Real-estate crowdfunding projects sometimes do this. The borrower buys the property, renovates it, and then refinances it using the equity to pay off lenders as well as themselves.

Whether you offer equity ownership or pay interest on a loan, put everything in writing. You don't always need an attorney or an accountant to create these agreements. For example, if you have two equity investors and yourself, you can easily create an LLC (see Chapter 10) where you retain, say, 60 percent ownership and give 20 percent to each investor. For a loan, online calculators make it easy for you and your lender to create a loan repayment schedule.

If the equity owners are passive investors and you do all of the work to maintain and manage the property, that simplifies things. But put everything in writing. Be clear on the roles and expectations for each investor. And seek professional help if you need it.

Once you obtain your investors, keep them informed. An email now and then will do. This will ease any anxiety they have about investing in your property. But be honest. If your property is experiencing some problems, your investors may be able to help. They want to see you succeed because they succeed, too.

If you can't raise enough money from friends and family, you may have to turn to a lending institution or seek funds from private or public investment sources (see Chapter 9). Those institutions will want to know how much money you raised from others and how much you owe.

As you know, too much debt can kill your chances of getting another loan. The No. 1 factor in obtaining a loan is the amount of income you have. You'll also need to have good credit. If you don't have good credit, there are some other options for obtaining loans through crowdfunding platforms. These are also discussed in Chapter 9.

What If Your Venture Fizzles?

As noted earlier in this chapter, family and friends are the most significant source of investment funds for new business ventures.

But before you collect cash from them, carefully consider what will happen to your personal relationships if your venture is a bust. (Not likely with real estate, but always possible.) Will they become angry and bitter toward you? Will it ruin your relationships for life?

Some people can separate the personal from the professional. They won't hold a grudge no matter what happens. But not many of us are that saintly. Is a $1,000 investment from a close friend worth risking your personal relationship with them?

That's a question only you can answer. If the person is really a good friend, why should a loss of $1,000 kill a friendship? But what about $2,000, $5,000 or more? The more people invest, the angrier they are likely to be if your rental property venture fails and they lose their money.

One way to limit the damage to your relationships with others is to ensure that the people who invest can do so comfortably. If your sister-in-law has trouble paying the rent every month, discourage her from giving you money. She may come back in six months and ask you for some of her money back, and if you don't have the financial resources to give it back, neither of you is going to be happy.

Some people believe you should never borrow money from a friend or family member. If you subscribe to this belief, don't despair. There are other sources of money out there, including professional investors, the topic of the next chapter.

Outside Investors as Assets

Your attempts to raise money from family and friends or obtain a federally backed mortgage loan have failed, and you don't have any equity in a property that you can tap.

All is not lost.

Consider raising capital from outside investors, which includes lending institutions and professional investors. I caution you, though, that this isn't easy to do. The Securities and Exchange Commission (SEC) has strict rules when it comes to raising capital from outside sources. Should you fail to follow those rules, you can be fined or even be sent to jail. But if you have a good business plan, you have a fighting chance to get some funding.

To raise capital through securities such as banknotes, bonds, stocks, futures, and options, you must follow rules pertaining to disclosure of information as well as registering with the SEC. This can be complicated and expensive, but there are some ways to reduce the burden.

In this chapter, I'll introduce you to some of the SEC rules and procedures you'll need to follow to obtain funding from outside sources. Note that these rules and procedures often change as SEC leadership changes. You'll also need to consult professional advice before embarking on a fund-raising campaign.

Although you may not be in a position to raise money from outside investors, I'm providing this information because down the road things might change. Being aware of your options is a good state of mind when it comes to running a business.

What Is a Security?

An effort to raise capital will qualify as a *security* when (1) investors expect to get a return on their money and when (2) they are passive investors, which means they are not involved with the activity that generates the profit or with the management of the business.

If someone gives you money and in return you give them a product or service, this normally is not a security. It's a business transaction. If your attempt to raise money qualifies as a security, you have to register it with the SEC.

Before accepting any money, you must provide "full disclosure" to investors of all material facts. A *material fact* is anything that investors would consider before investing in your venture, such as information about you, how the money will be spent, how your business will be managed, and how your investors will be paid. You'll need to create a prospectus using SEC guidelines and that agency must approve it before you solicit and accept funds.

This can be costly. If you want to sell stock in a company (called an Initial Public Offering, or IPO), the average yearly cost of everything (directors' fees, liability insurance, audit and securities compliance and related legal fees) is more than $3 million. You and your company also will have to comply with state laws, which can add to costs.

If your company fails and investors sue, you are not liable as long as you followed SEC rules and did not engage in fraud. However, if you violated those rules or laws, you may be required to pay back all of the money that was invested and you can be sent to jail.

Exceptions to Registering with the SEC

Because of the high cost of filing with the SEC, most entrepreneurs, especially those with new businesses or the need to raise capital for funding real estate ventures, seek to be exempted under SEC rules.[100] They are complicated, but here are some general guidelines:

- In general, an exemption is easier to get if you do not offer the sale of your securities to the public. The sale must be private and targeted mainly to accredited investors, who have the knowledge and financial resources to protect themselves. This is the way many big time real estate investors raise money for their ventures.

- Some rules allow you to sell securities to a limited number of non-accredited investors and to the public, but there are additional rules on doing this. They must be given disclosure documents and the names and addresses of the company's owners and promoters.

- Most of the exemptions limit the amount of investment money that can be raised, but in recent years the SEC continues to increase the amounts, which are as much as $75 million during a 12-month period.

You'll need to consult professionals before pursuing an exemption.

Principles for Approaching Investors

Raising capital from outside investors is difficult. It can take months to develop levels of confidence and trust necessary to obtain funding. There will be rejections.

---

[100]For more in-depth information about the exemptions, see "Exempt Offerings," U.S. Securities and Exchange Commission (no date), retrieved 12/31/23 from <https://www.sec.gov/education/capitalraising/exemptofferings>.

Below are eight principles or rules to help guide you. They apply whether you are seeking money from professional investors or from lending institutions.

1. *Know Your Weaknesses.* Successful entrepreneurs understand their weaknesses. For example, they hire someone else to do a job that they can't do.

2. *Have Clear Goals.* You have clear goals when you can answer this question: "How would you summarize in one sentence the mission or goal of your business or venture?"

   - Microsoft: *to empower every person and every organization on the planet to achieve more.*
   - Pinterest: *to help empower people to discover things they love and inspire them to go do those things in real life.*
   - Google: *to organize the world's information and make it universally accessible and useful.*
   - Amazon: *to continually raise the bar of the customer experience by using the internet and technology to help consumers find, discover and buy anything, and empower businesses and content creators to maximize their success.*

3. *Do Your Research.* Investors will not put money into a venture if they are not convinced it will produce a good return. Put together a detailed proposal that elaborates on costs, marketing, manpower, and management.

4. *Be Nice and Listen.* Ideally, you should be able to raise capital for your real estate venture based only on the merits of your proposal, not on how likable you are. But people are human, which means they like to connect emotionally to each other. If investors don't like you, they are going to be less likely to support your project. So, before talking

business, talk about the weather, sports, or the successes of your potential funders. Stay away from politics. That will kill a deal very quickly. Ask questions about them and their lives. Make them feel important. And one way to do that is to listen to them. Do not turn the conversation back to you. Keep it on them. In due time they will get to your proposal.

5. *Keep Your Pitch Short.* Some consultants say it should be no longer than 15 to 20 minutes, or 20 slides or pages. Focus on the market, your team, and financial projections. Of course, you'll have to put together a longer, written presentation. Spice it up with graphics and visuals that enhance understanding.

6. *Return on Investment More Is Important than Cost.* In terms of obtaining funding, remember that *the total cost of your project is far less important than expected return on investment.* Investors aren't looking for the cheapest deal possible, they are looking for the deal that will produce the highest return.

7. *Tell Stories.* One of my journalism teachers told me many decades ago, "David, teach by example or anecdote. That's how students remember things." In other words, tell stories when you are pitching your venture. Stories have a beginning, a middle, and an end. Use stories to emphasize a particular point or argument. Investors will remember your stories, and people who remember are more likely to fund your project.

8. *Follow up.* Investors are busy people and it normally will take some time for them to feel comfortable investing in your business. Send an email or text after a meeting. Calling is also an option, but sometimes a phone call is too inconvenient. Keep them informed. If they aren't interested, then try another set of investors. They may not be interested in this venture, but maybe they will for the next.

Crowdfunding

Crowdfunding is the practice of funding a venture by raising small amounts of money from a large number of people, usually through the internet. Crowdfunding ventures raise about $1.4 billion every year for millions of campaigns, according to Statista.[101] About 20 percent of campaigns are successful. Many crowdfunding platforms require fund-raisers to reach a goal before funding a project.

Many crowdfunding projects are rewards-based, which involves giving investors a gift or product for investing as opposed to interest payments or equity. Most crowdfunding sites make their money by charging a percentage of the funds raised.

Some crowdfunding sites are used to raise money for medical expenses for a person or to fund a charity. GoFundMe is a popular site for this type of fund-raising. But a few crowdfunding sites cater to entrepreneurs who are trying to raise money for ventures. Such projects sometimes involve clearance through the SEC.

Two sites that can cater to real estate investors are Crowdfunder and WeFunder.[102]

Crowdfunder offers equity crowdfunding, which means that entrepreneurs sell shares of their company to accredited investors. The site has raised more than $150 million from 12,000 venture capitalists and angel investors.

WeFunder allows entrepreneurs to raise between $50,000 and $50 million from investors. Projects range from funding a restaurant to

---

[101]"Market Size of Crowdfunding Worldwide in 2022 and 2023 with a Forecast for 2030," Statista (2023), retrieved 12/29/23 from <https://www.statista.com/statistics/1078273/global-crowdfunding-market-size>.

[102]"12 Best Crowdfunding Sites For Small Business," Fresh Books Cloud Accounting, retrieved 9/ 30/ 20, from <https://www.freshbooks.com/hub/startup/small-business-crowdfunding>.

technology start-ups. WeFunder has more than 150,000 investors. Investors pay fees to WeFunder.

If you raise money through a crowdfunding site, you are expected to follow through on your promises. If you say you are going to use the money for a real estate venture but use it for personal reasons, you can be charged with fraud and jailed.

Angel Investors

An angel investor is a person who has financial resources and provides money for a business start-up and receives an ownership equity in the venture. Many angels invest through crowdfunding sites.

Angel investments are risky and, consequently, require a high return. If your real estate venture is expected to produce only a modest return, your chances of obtaining an angel are lessened. Many angels want a 15+ percent return in five years. They often invest more than $50,000.

Angels inhabit the space between amateur investors (friends and family) and professional investors (venture capitalists). Angel investors can be found on crowdfunding sites, although many are more comfortable funding local projects. Every major city has angel investors, who are connected into various networks of other angels and business associates in a community. Your business colleagues, attorneys, accountants, and bankers will know them.

Part IV

How to Create Your Real Estate Company

Unincorporated Forms of Business

You have raised the capital you need to buy or invest in a rental property, so the next step is to create a business entity if you haven't already done that.

The most popular forms of small business organization are *sole proprietorships, partnerships,* and *limited liability companies.* All three are *unincorporated* businesses, which means they're not legally separate from their owners.

In contrast, a *corporation* is a legal entity separate from its owners, who are called shareholders. The organization is controlled by a board of directors who oversee management, who typically also are shareholders. Corporations give their owners limited liability protection, which means they are financially responsible only for the money they invest, not for the business's debts. In other words, if the business goes belly up, its creditors cannot take the personal assets of shareholders to pay the debts.

The LLC and some forms of partnership offer limited liability to owners, too. And they are much easier to create. If your investors want some equity ownership in your real estate venture, you should create a partnership or a limited liability company. On the other hand, if they loan you money, you could stick with a sole proprietorship.

This chapter shows you how to create an unincorporated company.

The next chapter shows you how to create an incorporated business, such as a C corporation and S corporation. These latter two choices are almost never used for small business ventures, because they require substantial investment capital. But as your business grows, you may convert yours into one of them, so I will provide a brief discussion of how they work.

Sole Proprietorships

The sole proprietorship is the easiest form of business to create, because you don't have to do anything. You are the business.

There are no federal or state requirements. You don't even have to open a separate business checking account.

When customers purchase a product or service from you, they make the check out to you in your name or give you the cash in person or through a Venmo or Zelle payment, which goes directly into your personal account. Clean and simple.

But one of the biggest disadvantages of a sole proprietorship is lack of protection for your personal assets. If your business generates a lot of debt, your creditors can go after all of your personal assets, including your home, car, jewelry, and other valuables. Sole proprietorship works well with people who run businesses that aren't likely to generate debts or liability lawsuits, such as home cleaning services.

But if you have a mortgage on your rental property, you may be forced to operate as a sole proprietorship.

The Mortgage Problem

In the field of rental real estate, most entrepreneurs prefer to create an LLC or partnership, which offer protection for their personal assets. When they purchase a house, they ideally do so through their LLC.

However, if you already own your rental home and have a mortgage on it, the lender may not allow you to transfer the deed from your name into your LLC. If you do that, the company could demand full repayment on the mortgage, because the mortgage is under your name, not the LLC. There are ways to overcome this problem, but you will need to hire an attorney and it could cost you thousands of collars.[103]

A better method of transferring ownership to an LCC is to pay off the mortgage and then change the deed to your name. But because it is now a business, the lending institutions will treat you as a business, which means you typically will be paying higher interest rates if you use that property as collateral for a loan.[104]

If you are concerned about liability lawsuits on your rental property, there is another option. *Carry a lot of landlord insurance.* Some real estate attorneys even advise that insurance is a far better protection than an LLC. Of course, both might offer the best protection.

One more comment. If you are more concerned about protecting your personal assets from creditors, creating an LLC may offer you some protection. However, it depends on whether you create the company before or after the debts build up. If the latter, the bankruptcy court may see your actions as an attempt to skirt financial responsibility to your creditors, and you will lose your limited liability protection.

Taxes, DBA, and EIN

As a sole proprietorship, you will pay income taxes on rental income you earn, including FICA payments. You must keep track of income and

---

[103]Richard Keyt, "How Do I Transfer Real Estate to My LLC?" Keyt Law LLC Attorneys (undated), retrieved 1/22/24 from <https://www.keytlaw.com/azllclaw/2017/01/transfer-real-estate-to-llc>.

[104]Small businesses are typically charged higher interest rates because they are considered to be higher risk than mortgage loans to homeowners.

expenditures and report that information on your federal and state income tax forms. On the federal form, it's Schedule C, Business Income and Expenditures. Your Social Security number can be used as your tax ID number (see Chapter 20).

If you decide (or are forced) to operate as a sole proprietorship, you can operate your business under a separate business name, such as "Dave's Property Management." This is called an *assumed name* or a *doing business as name* (DBA). You can obtain a separate tax ID number for the business, which is a good idea to protect the privacy of your Social Security number. You typically file this business name with your secretary of state, department of state, or a corporation commission office. When customers pay you, they write a check to your DBA, which you deposit into your DBA checking account.

To open that account, your financial institution will ask you for your driver's license or personal identification card, as well as the official state records showing that you own the DBA registration and your Social Security number or your Employee Identification Number (EIN). If you have employees, you'll need to create an EIN, because it's required by the IRS. The EIN is simple to obtain (see Step 5 later in this chapter under the heading "Creating a Limited Liability Company").

Even if you don't have employees, I recommend you obtain an EIN anyway, because it means you don't have to reveal your Social Security number when you send 1099 forms to non-employee contractors who work for you or when you provide customers with a W-9 form, which gives them information about your business so they can pay you. The government collects this information to ensure you are not fabricating expenses.

Although you don't have to file paperwork to create an SP, you may need a permit or license from various federal, state, or local governments to sell or trade in certain products and services.

The big advantage of the SP is that it is easy to set up, easy to file your taxes, and low maintenance, both in terms of little or no paperwork to file with the government and cost (an attorney or accountant often is not needed until the business becomes bigger).

The big disadvantage is that if one of your customers gets hurt on your property, or you accidentally hurt someone on the job, or your business is sued for violating a law or failing to pay a debt, the injured party or the government can confiscate your personal assets, such as your car, home or bank account. The best way to protect against this is to always pay your bills, follow the law, and carry adequate liability to protect yourself against injury lawsuits.

Partnerships

Your auntie gives you some investment money and says she wants an equity stake in your business, but you still want to control everything. A limited liability partnership can accommodate both of you.

Auntie gets limited liability, which means that she will not be responsible for any excess debts your partnership creates. She and you can only lose the amounts you invest, not your personal assets. But you assume full responsibility for the debts. This gives auntie confidence that you will do your best to manage the business in a responsible manner.

There are five types of partnerships, not all of which are offered in every state: general partnership (GP), limited partnership (LP), master limited partnership (MLP), limited liability partnership (LLP), and limited liability limited partnership (LLLP).

General Partnership

A general partnership is a sole proprietorship with two or more people who agree to share in the assets, profits, and financial and legal liabilities of a business. Like a sole proprietorship, the partners do not get unlimited liability, which means they are personally responsible for all debts and liabilities of the organization.

Like a sole proprietorship (SP), a GP does not have to file any paperwork with the state. The company emerges when the partners begin doing business. They are taxed as individuals. But they don't have to open a separate bank account or keep business income and expenses separate from personal expenses and income unless they create a DBA.

Although a general partnership doesn't have to create or submit formal paperwork to the state, it's a good idea to put in writing how the partnership will be managed, the roles of each partner, and how profits will be distributed. Misunderstandings can create big problems.

Partnerships often dissolve when one partner leaves the business or one dies or becomes disabled. But the business can continue if provisions for such conditions are made in advance.

Limited Partnership

A limited partnership may be the best choice for auntie and you.

You are the general partner who controls the business and auntie is a limited partner who is granted limited liability, which means her personal assets cannot be confiscated to pay business debts. However, as the general partner, you don't have limited liability. You will have to pay the debts of the business and your personal assets can be tapped to do this. This liability gives your investors more confidence in you, because you will pay a big price if the venture fails.

On the income auntie receives from the partnership, she will pay the lower capital gains tax rates rather than the higher earned income tax rates. The LP can be used for short-term projects (such as buying property), but it also can continue into perpetuity. However, the illness or death of one of the partners often triggers dissolution.

Limited partnerships, unlike general partnerships, usually must register with the state. This is necessary so that limited partners may obtain limited liability. Limited partnerships also may have to file an annual report with the state.

Master Limited Partnership

The limited partners in a master limited partnership (MLP) can trade their ownership like equities to other investors. The limited partners enjoy limited liability and their profits are taxed at the lower capital gains rate. Only businesses that deal in natural resources, which includes real estate, can create an MLP. Ninety percent of the company's income must come from things like energy pipelines and storage, commodities, or real estate. The term "master" in the MLP refers to the general partner, who typically owns only a small percentage of the company. The master can buy additional shares as a limited partner and earns a salary that is taxed at the higher earned income rate.

Limited Liability Partnership

Limited liability partnerships can only be created by professionals such as accountants, architects, attorneys, dentists, and doctors. The LLP offers partners limited liability. But the LLP cannot protect them from liability that stems from their personal acts, such as malpractice. Liability insurance is the best protection here.

Limited Liability Limited Partnership

The limited liability limited partnership is offered in at least 30 states and consists of one or more general partners who can transfer liability to an external insurer.

Most LLLPs are created from existing limited partnerships. LPs with general partners can dissolve the general partner and replace it with an individual limited partner. Real estate investment businesses often use this form of organization. You should consult with an attorney if you decide to create an LLLP, because they aren't recognized in all states.

Limited Liability Companies

A limited liability company (LLC) contains elements of both the sole proprietorship and the regular corporation. LLC owners benefit from limited liability but for tax purposes are treated just like owners of sole proprietorships. The IRS doesn't even formally recognize the LLC as a taxable entity. Only the owners are taxed.

The LLC is the second most popular form of business organization in America, behind the sole proprietorship (22 million v. 23 million, respectively).[105] One person can create an LLC. It's easy to set up and the profits are not double-taxed, as they are at corporations. Corporate profits are taxed at the corporate level and then again when the profits are distributed to individual shareholders. Only the owners of LLCs are taxed.

LLCs can include more than one owner and the members can hire a nonowner to manage the company. The only downside of an LLC is that the owners' profits are taxed as earned income, not capital gains. As such, the effective tax rate can be twice as high if you're a high-income earner. The lower your income, the smaller the difference between earned income tax rates and capital gains rates.

---

[105]"Is It Time to Think about an LLC for Your Business?" Fitzpatrick, Lentz & Bubba (March 2, 2021), retrieved 12/28/23 from <https://www.flblaw.com/is-it-time-to-think-about-an-llc-for-your-business>.

You don't need an attorney or accountant to create an LLC. All you need is a business name (like "Dave's Properties LLC") and then you file with your state. Although all free-market countries around the world offer limited liability forms of business, not all allow one person to form and own an LLC, as does the United States.[51] Some require at least two members. LLCs are regulated by the states, usually through the secretary of state, a corporation commission, or a commerce department. Most states require a small fee to create the LLC. (California is an exception; it charges $800.)

Creating a Limited Liability Company

To register your business name as an LLC, go online and type this in a search bar: "Create an LLC in (fill in your state's name)." Ignore the "dot com" websites, because they want to charge you to file the form. You can do it on your own at no charge. Look for a **.gov** listing.

Each state has a different set of rules for completing LLC applications. But here are some of the basic steps.

1. Pick a Name and an Agent

Create a business name that represents the image you want to project to customers. Make it professional. Add LLC to the end of your chosen name. When you insert that name, most sites will search their records to see if that name is already taken in your state. If it is, just modify it or pick another name.

At the same time, you typically will identify a registered or statutory agent who will serve as the point of contact for your company. You can do it yourself or hire a firm that specializes in representing companies. The former doesn't cost you anything.

The state, individuals who want to contact you, and other institutions (such as the courts) will mail all legal and nonlegal documents to the agent and address you provide. You can use your home address. But note that some states require you to be at your address during business hours. If a lawsuit plaintiff tries to serve papers and you aren't there, the court could issue a default judgment against you.

2. File Articles of Organization

Most states will create the Articles of Organization for you.

You first decide whether the LLC will be *member-managed* or *manager-managed.* The former means that the members of the LLC (or just you) will manage the company, whereas the latter means you will hire someone to manage the business and you and other members will be passive owners.

If you are the only member of the LLC, then choose the member-managed option. The state will create and send you the Articles of Organization after you pay the required fee. If you have one or more investors, consider creating an operating agreement to ensure that all business owners understand how the LLC is going to be operated and managed.

Some states allow you to select the web page address (Uniform Resource Locator) for your business. You'll set that up with a web hosting service provider, such as GoDaddy or Bluehost. Be sure the one you want is available before you file your business name. Contact a business attorney or accountant if you have questions.

3. Register with Local Governments

You may have to register your business with the state, city, or jurisdiction in which you will operate. Check with your local governmental and state commerce entity or secretary of state.

4. Obtain an Employer Identification Number

When you file your taxes, you can use your Social Security number or apply for an Employer Identification Number, commonly called EIN. Using an EIN will makes it impossible for unscrupulous people to steal your Social Security number.

The IRS issues the EIN at no charge. Just search "Apply for EIN," or follow this link (https://www.irs.gov/businesses/small-businesses-self-employed/apply-for-an-employer-identification-number-ein-online). Once again, be wary of online sites that will trick you into thinking you're on the **.gov** site. They charge $50 or more for an EIN, but it's free at the link above.

5. Open a Business Checking Account

You'll need a checking account to run your new company.

The bank or credit union will need your driver's license (or passport), LLC paperwork (provided by the state), tax identification number (if applicable), and Social Security number. The law requires lending institutions to obtain this information.

For an initial deposit, write a check from your personal checking account and make it out to your LLC. If you deposit large sums of money (e.g., $10,000+), the lending institution may require you to document the source of the funds. The law requires these financial institutions to report money laundering or other suspicious activity.

You should also consider ordering some business cards and perhaps some stationery. Add "LLC" at the end. That can sound awkward, but it will protect you against veil-piercing lawsuits (see discussion later in this chapter). Online printers offer these products for nominal charges.

6. File an Annual Report

Most states require owners of LLCs to file annual reports usually at the end of the year or around tax time. If you don't file one, the state or government entity could revoke your LLC charter.

Piercing the Corporate Veil

To keep your personal assets protected, follow the laws and rules that govern LLCs in your state. The key is that your business must be a separate entity from you, which means that you should:

1. Never engage in illegal or fraudulent activities.
2. Keep your records up to date.
3. Don't mix personal and business monies; keep separate checking accounts.
4. Always file paperwork and pay fees required by state or federal law.
5. Always use or include the "LLC" when referring to your company (this keeps your business entity separate from your personal entity).
6. Hold an annual meeting at least once a year, even if your state doesn't require one. The meeting doesn't need to long or formal, but create some minutes to address some of the issues or goals facing your company.
7. Consult an attorney when you need legal advice.

If you fail to follow these rules, a court can issue an order that removes the "veil" of legal protection provided by your LLC. You will then have to use your personal assets to satisfy a judgment against you and/or your LLC.

Incorporated Forms of Business

If your real estate business has been growing rapidly and you are in a high-income bracket, you might consider converting your general partnership or limited liability company into a C or S corporation.

This can lower your taxes. The rental income you receive from your company currently is taxed as earned income, which can be as high as 37 percent. If you incorporate, your income would be taxed as a capital gain, which puts the ceiling at about 20 percent.

A corporate form of organization also would allow you to avoid paying taxes on *retained income*, or profits that are not distributed. That money typically is set aside to pay for future purchases or investments.

With a GP or LLC, each owner or partner pays taxes on the money even though they do not actually receive it. A corporation skirts this problem. Another advantage of a corporation is that it allows shareholders to easily transfer their ownership (stock) in the company.

One major disadvantage to creating a regular corporation (also called a C corporation) is double-taxation: once on corporate profits and once again when shareholders sell their stock and/or dividends.

But there's a way around this problem for owners of smaller companies. An S corporation is not double-taxed. It fills that spot in-between an LLC and the C corporation, at least in terms of tax benefits. Profits are only taxed once at the lower capital gains tax rate. Your profit depends on how much stock you own.

The C or S corporation is a good option when you need lots of investors to fund a multimillion-dollar business or project. That's because investors want their income from the project to be taxed as capital gains, not as earned income, which is subject to FICA taxes.

The C and S corporation both have the same organizational structure. The S corporation is actually a designation of the IRS, which gives smaller corporations special tax advantages. In exchange for those advantages, the S corporation can only have up to 100 shareholders. The purpose is to help smaller corporations thrive.

I'll talk about the C corporation first, because both types of corporations have the same general structure.

The C Corporation

A corporation has four major characteristics:

1. It's a legal entity independent of its owners.
2. It offers limited liability to its shareholders.
3. Its organizational structure tends to be complex.
4. It has shareholders and a board of directors.

Like other forms of business, the states establish the rules for forming a corporation. Most experts recommend small-business owners establish corporations in their home states, but they don't have to do that. Most public corporations are incorporated in Delaware, which has a reputation as being business-friendly because of its tax law and special court system specifically for corporate legal cases.[106]

---

[106]Charlotte Morabito, "Here's Why more than 60% of Fortune 500 Companies Are Incorporated in Delaware," CNBC (March 13, 2023), retrieved 1/22/24 from <https://www.cnbc.com/2023/03/13/why-more-than-60percent-of-fortune-500-companies-incorporated-in-delaware.html>.

To create a corporation, you'll register a business name, file a certificate of incorporation or articles of incorporation, pay a fee to the state, and draft corporate bylaws and rules for conducting a board of directors meeting.

As of this writing, corporations pay a flat 21 percent tax on their profits to the federal government. But corporations can deduct a lot of expenses. This includes employee wages, compensation for officers, bad debts, depreciation, repairs and maintenance, rents, profit-sharing, and employee, health insurance and pensions, and charitable donations.

Your corporation may offer stock to the public, to its employees, or to private investors. The board of directors controls the company, not the owner or person who created it. This means that a corporation, unlike a single-owner LLC, survives the death of its owner.

To create a corporation, you'll need help from legal, accounting, and business advisers. The more stock you sell and the higher the price, the more revenue you will have to invest or to pay expenses. You also can issue dividends to shareholders, which can draw in more investors. But that reduces the size of the investment pool.

Forming a corporation is similar to creating an LLC. You need to:

1. Select a corporate name (Inc. goes at the end), one whose trademark or service mark is available.
2. Draft and file articles of incorporation that include, among other things, the amount and type of stock (e.g., common or preferred) being issued.
3. Create corporate bylaws.
4. Draft a shareholder agreement that identifies who can become a new shareholder and how they can sell their shares.
5. Maintain a record of corporate minutes.
6. Issue shares of stock and identify who owns them and how many shares are outstanding.
7. Obtain an EIN and decide whether you want to file as an S corporation.
8. Obtain required licenses and permits.

The S Corporation

An S corporation is a tax designation created by the IRS. It's not a unique form of organization. It's just taxed at a lower rate than C corporations and LLCs.

As noted above, the profits from an S corporation are taxed only when they pass through to the shareholders, who also pay the lower capital gains rate. An S corporation also can offer some benefits not available to LLCs, including tax deductions for health insurance and disability.

The purpose of the S tax designation is to help small businesses thrive. But there are restrictions on size and who can be a shareholder. Below I present some of the key ones. Visit the IRS website to see all of the rules.

1. Only domestic companies are eligible, not international ones.
2. Shareholders must be individuals or part of trusts and estates. Partnerships, corporations, or non-resident aliens cannot own stock.
3. The maximum number of shareholders is 100.
4. The company can only offer one class of stock, not two (either common or preferred stock).
5. Some insurance companies, financial institutions, and domestic international sales corporations are prohibited from forming S corporations.

If you are an employee and shareholder of the company, the IRS requires your company to pay you a "reasonable salary" before paying yourself a tax-free distribution. Your salary must be similar to those of presidents at other companies with similar revenues. Of course, with a higher salary, you'll be paying more in taxes (FICA and higher earned income tax bracket).

Although S corporation status means you pay less federal taxes, that status may not apply to state taxes. Some states don't recognize the tax advantages of an S corporation and will treat your company as a C corporation.

Be aware, too, that power in an S or C corporation depends in part on how many shares a person or organization owns. Although you may have established the corporation, if you fall into disfavor with the board of directors or shareholders, you can be pushed out.

Part V

How to Buy a Good Rental Property

Picking the Right Market

If you don't own a house that you can convert into a rental, then this chapter is for you. And even if you own a rental, if you intend to buy another one sometime soon, this chapter is also for you. It shows you how to find the ideal market and house.

This process of buying a rental property involves a little bit of science and a lot of art. There isn't a simple formula that one can use. There are too many variables and factors affecting the buying process.

But that doesn't mean the process is capricious. There are a number of things you should look for, and I'll use my first condo purchase to illustrate some of these criteria.

Recall from Chapter 1 that I purchased my first property while I was ghostwriting a real estate book for Ken McElroy, a prominent real estate entrepreneur in Scottsdale who had nearly a billion dollars of property under his company's management. Ken is an amiable man, a good father, and a respected employer. I enjoyed working with him and his staff.

Before I started writing his book, I read several other books he had published. The first thought that came to my mind: *Why didn't I get into real estate 20 years ago?* I could have been a wealthy real estate mogul today.

Well, maybe not.

But I don't regret my career as a journalist and professor. Writing, family, and friends are my passion. Nothing can replace that. However, I did desire a few more dollars coming in to make my retired life a bit easier.

So I decided to purchase a property while I was writing the book. And my first choice for a market was Sun City, Arizona, which is located on the west side of the Phoenix metropolitan area. Sun City is where many people from northern states retire. Some commute, staying in Arizona during the winter and living back home in the summer.

Guidelines for Picking the Market

Note that I haven't said a thing yet about the property I bought. That's because the building itself is far less important than the market when you are buying a rental, a point Ken has made in his books and one that I, too, made early in this book. Let me repeat it again.

The market is more important than the building
when it comes to buying rental properties.

A good house in a bad market is not a good investment. If the values of the homes in that market are declining, the value of your rental property will decline, too. And that means your property will not appreciate much over the long haul. Appreciation is the biggest factor driving profitability of a rental property when the mortgage is still being paid off.

A poor house in a good market, on the other hand, is a good investment. You can fix it up and easily rent it. People want to live in nice areas, not in slum areas even if the house there is nice.

So how do you find a good market?

McElroy's Three Drivers of Supply and Demand

In his books, podcasts, and videos, Ken points out that three factors drive supply and demand for rental properties: *employment, resources,* and *location.*[107]

1. *Employment.* People move to areas where the jobs are. Renters like to be close to where they work. Homeowners will drive farther because affordable housing is often in outlying boundaries of a city. These areas typically are not good markets for rental housing.

2. *Resources.* Places with natural and human-created resources are good places for rental properties. The short-term rental condos at Mission Beach in San Diego draw lots of visitors, as do the ski slopes in Colorado and the golf courses and shopping malls in Arizona. Institutions like universities, high tech businesses, casinos, and miliary bases also have a high demand for housing, but note that if they close down, the tenants will leave and you, as a landlord, can lose your shirt. Buying in an economically diverse area is wise.

3. *Location.* The area around your property can also affect demand for housing. Such is the case if your property has what Ken calls "drive-by visibility," which allows you to pitch a "For Rent" sign that saves you advertising expenses. You also need to look at crime and poverty rate statistics for the area. These are available from city, state, and national websites. Although some real estate investors have gotten rich renting properties in poor areas, they take on a lot of management problems and headaches. The biggest problem, though, is that property values in high crime/high poverty areas don't appreciate as quickly and you may have more difficulty selling your property.

---

[107]Ken McElroy, *ABCs of Buying Rental Property: How You Can Achieve Financial Freedom in Five Years* (Scottsdale, AZ: KM Press, 2020; 2nd printing).

I knew Sun City was a good market for my rental after reading Ken's books. I also figured that it would be a good market for a short-term rental. Many people like to vacation in Arizona during the winter. After all, the sun shines 87 percent of the time.

Short-term rentals can be expensive in the Phoenix and Scottsdale areas during peak season. But properties in Sun City can offer lower rates, because the homes there cost less and the property taxes are lower. The recreational facilities in Sun City are also top notch: eight golf courses, six swimming pools, four fitness facilities, 30 bowling lanes, a lake, miniature golf, and lots of arts and crafts clubs.

Of course, there were some disadvantages to buying in Sun City.

New buyers at that time had to pay a $3,500 one-time "Preservation & Improvement" fee and a $300 ownership transfer fee. Owners also had to pay an Annual Property Assessment of $496, which enabled them or their renters to use the many recreational facilities in the community. But these costs are depreciable or tax deductible for landlords, so that takes some of the sting out of them.

Just before I bought my property in Sun City, I didn't know much about community itself. How much did a typical home or condo cost? Were the values increasing? I found a lot of this information at websites like Zillow.com, Realtor.com, and Trulia.com.

In the search bar, I typed "Property values in Sun City Arizona."

Zillow was the first listing (ignoring all of the advertisement listings before it). The website makes much of its money from real estate firms and agents who advertise to pick up new buyers. Be forewarned, though, if you click on a link to see more about the property, you won't be taken to the listing agent, you'll be shunted to an agent looking for a buyer. They won't be able to answer your questions without doing research on their own.

At any rate, Zillow listed Sun City as a "very hot" market, which meant is was a seller's market. At the time, there were more buyers than sellers, and so prices were higher.[108] But don't let that scare you away.

In January 2019, the median home sale price in Sun City was $168,000 — 24 percent less than home values in the entire Phoenix metropolitan area. Over the previous eight years, prices on the average property had increased 119 percent, from $76,600 to $168,000. That's an annualized gain of 10.3 percent per year.

The median rent price in Sun City was $1,288 (about 90 cents per square foot), compared to $1,595 for the rest of the Phoenix metropolitan area.

I found another website called "Neighborhood Scout" that provided information about demographics, real estate, crime, and schools. As expected, crime was low in the area, partly because younger people don't live there. In general, people commit fewer crimes as they age.

Trulia, another online site (owned by Zillow), also showed that rent rates increased 9 percent ($100 a month) from June to August. So the going monthly rate when I purchased was $1,300.

Many other websites provide information about Sun City, but you get the picture. You can learn a lot about a market in just an hour of research on the internet.

Assessing the Quality of a Market

You will need a good real estate agent to buy your property.

But before you hire one, do some market research on your own, like I did. Some agents specialize in certain areas of a city, and you will want to pick an agent who has a lot of knowledge about the market areas you are investigating.

And to help you pick those areas, I've got a list of questions in Table 12.1 on the next page. This shouldn't be the only criterion you use to

---

[108]Data retrieved 10/3/2019 from <https://www.zillow.com/sun-city-az/home-values>.

Table 12.1

Assessing the Quality of a Rental Market

Is the market area or community ...	No <------> Yes		
1. Clean and attractive? Are there junk cars or untidy lawns or yards? Is there graffiti on common area walls and buildings? Are there a lot of abandoned commercial buildings?	-1	0	1
2. Safe? What do the local violent crime statistics show?	-1	0	1
3. Served by good K-12 schools? Good schools are especially important for parents who are educated and looking to buy a home. Go to GreatSchools.org and look up the ratings on the schools in the market area. An 8+ is a "1"; 5-7 is "0"; 4 and below is "-1."	-1	0	1
4. Populated with homes/condos whose values are increasing? Check stories in papers or county assessor's office.	-2	0	2
5. Served by restaurants, shopping malls, supermarkets, and recreational facilities (like golf courses, ball diamonds, parks, universities)?	-1	0	1
6. Quiet? Is there an airport, light rail, train or bus station nearby?	-1	0	1
7. Filled with shopping centers with few vacancies and few payday loan, title loan, thrift store, and strip joints?	-1	0	1
8. Filled with businesses that offer good paying jobs?	-1	0	1
9. Close to where most people work? Suburban communities often are not good places for renters, who prefer being closer to work.	-1	0	1
10. Suffering from a shortage of rental units?	-2	0	2
Question if you plan to have a short-term rental: **11. Does the market attract tourists, or are there some natural resources** (like lakes for recreation, or sunshine and warm weather in the winter, or snow skiing in the winter) **or spectacular views of mountains, oceans, or lakes?**	-2	0	2
SUM OF THE RESPONSES (plus score indicates a good market)			

decide where to buy a property. But the questions should be helpful. Some reflect Ken's suggestions above.

The ideal market is one in which the community is clean, attractive, safe, served by good K-12 schools, and has access to shopping areas and recreational facilities. Most important of all, you need to determine whether the homes and condos in the area have been increasing in value over the past 10 years or so (I give this item a little more weight than the other items in Table 12.1). If not, your investment will not grow.

Ideally, you should look for markets where the supply of rental housing is low and demand is high (I give more weight to this question, too). You can determine the amount of supply in an area by examining tax and building records. Demand can be measured by looking at occupancy rates in cities and neighborhoods. Where rates are high, demand also tends to be high. In addition, if a lot of apartment complexes in the area are offering special prices for new move-ins, that can be an indicator that demand is soft and the supply of housing is too high.

The U.S. Census publishes statistics on occupancy rates by city.[109] Although the statistics aren't searchable by zip code area, they are available for cities. The data showed that for Phoenix, vacancy rates were relatively stable from 2015 to 2018, but rates declined substantially in Tucson because the number of new housing and apartment units declined.[110]

The supply side of the equation is less crucial when searching for a short-term rental, which typically is located in an area where the supply

---

[109]"2018 Housing Vacancy Survey Annual Statistics," U.S. Census Bureau (April 04, 2019), retrieved 12/29/23 from <https://www.census.gov/newsroom/press-releases/2019/hvs.html>.

[110]"Tucson, Arizona," U.S. Department of Housing and Urban Development Office of Policy Development and Research, Comprehensive Housing Market Analysis (April 1, 2016), retrieved 12/29/23 from <https://www.huduser.gov/portal/publications/pdf/TucsonAZ-comp-16.pdf>.

of housing is already high. Areas that draw tourists typically have a lot of rental units. Don't let that scare you away, because these areas often need more rental units.

But, if you are looking to rent short term, be sure to buy a property that you know can turn a profit for you on a long-term lease. The short-term rental market is extremely competitive and volatile. If your property fails as a short-term rental, you will need to rent it out long term. I will show you in the next chapter how to calculate the profitability of a property.

Picking the Right Property

Once you narrow down your markets, you'll need to hire a real estate agent to search for a specific rental property if you don't already have one in mind.

But take your time in finding the right agent.

Ideally, you want someone who is familiar with the markets you have selected. In a big city, agents typically specialize in local areas, not the entire area. They don't have enough time to understand all of the markets.

Ask friends, business associates, and relatives for referrals. The same goes for other people you hire. Referrals are far more reliable than online ratings, as long as they are objective.

And when your agent starts looking, be sure you can rent homes or condos long-term and short-term in the areas you are looking. Deed covenants and HOA rules often restrict owners from renting their property, especially short-term. Most single-family home areas are not under such restrictions, but be sure to check.

Although Sun City isn't very friendly toward short-term rentals, there's an upside to this. The supply of short-term rentals is low and, thus, demand is high. This is ideal if you can find a good property. Less competition means more chance of success.

But the ability to rent a property is only one of the many factors that need to be considered before buying. The single-most important factor is whether you can turn a profit on the property. I'll show you how to estimate your profits shortly. First, let's cover some other factors that affect the buying process.

Fixer-Upper or Not?

Do you want to buy a turn-key property or a fixer-upper?

A *turn-key* is ready to rent as is. It won't require a lot of fixing up or remodeling. If you don't have the time or the skills to make repairs, then a turn-key is probably your best option. The only downside is that you typically have to pay more for a house that is in good condition. Sellers factor that into the price.

You also have to decide whether you're going to manage the property yourself or hire a management company. Fees vary, but most will charge 15 percent to 25 percent of gross revenues. You also have to pay cleaning fees. These fees are a significant expense for a short-term rental. You'll have to make sure you can swing a profit with these added costs.

Many novice and experienced landlords like to fix houses up, partly because (1) they enjoy the work, (2) their costs are much lower than hiring professional companies, (3) they can get a lower price for a fixer-upper property, and (4) they will be able to sell it at a higher price after it's fixed.

Distance from Your Home or Business

Some real estate investors buy rental properties in other cities or states. They hire management companies to manage the properties. They are known as *absentee landlords*.

Although absentee landlordship can work well for large apartment complexes and experienced investors, it's typically not ideal for the new landlord with only one home or condo. In fact, if you live more than an hour away from your property, you'll find that it can be a great inconvenience, especially if a pipe breaks or a garage door stops working. That's two hours added to your time each trip.

My rental in Sun City was no more than 20 minutes away, which enabled me to respond quickly to problems. Of course, if you live far away from the rental, you could farm out the work to maintenance and repair professionals in the area of the rental property. But this will cost more. Some landlords have a select list of repair people whom they use and call on regularly. This also enables them to take vacations and time away from home. Your tenants or guests can call these individuals directly if they have problems.

In addition, you will want to search around for professionals who charge reasonable fees. Companies that advertise on television often are the most expensive. After all, they have to pay for those expensive ads.

The Noise Factor

Is the property you'd like to buy located close to an airport, light rail, train, busy highway, or bus station?

Noise can be a factor when renters choose a place to live. It's true that renters tend to be less picky when it comes to noise than homeowners. That's one of the reasons why you see so many apartment complexes next to freeways.

However, if you choose a property that comes with a lot of external noise, be prepared to drop the rental rate a little to keep it occupied. Even renters expect a little compensation when they are inconvenienced by something.

Swimming Pool, Hot Tub, Grilling Area

Do you want or need a house with a swimming pool, hot tub, or grilling area?

One of the main reasons people stay at my short-term rental home is the large swimming pool in the backyard. Guests also like the fact that I don't charge to heat the pool[111] in the winter, when night time temperatures in Phoenix often dip into the low 40s and even the 30s.

But a swimming pool is extra work and cost. Some long-term renters may like it, but you need to charge $150 to $300 more a month just to cover the pool chemicals and maintenance of the pool.

Same goes with a hot tub. Very popular item for short-term rentals. But they can be costly to maintain and are not standard items in long-term rental homes. One advantage of renting a condo is that they often offer community pools and hot tubs, along with exercise facilities, so you don't have to maintain these facilities. But you'll have to pay an HOA fee, which can easily exceed $200 a month.

Both of my short-term rentals had grills. Quite frankly, they are pain in the butt to clean. Some guests have left them a mess. So I put a note on the front page of the guest book asking them to clean the grill if used. The interesting thing is that few guests now use the grill. If the property has an outdoor grilling area, that can add extra time to the cleaning process. However, it's almost expected for high-end short-term rentals.

Garage, Carport, or Open Air?

A garage is not a necessity in Arizona, where many people have carports or just park on a driveway or street. It doesn't rain here often

---

[111]It has a heat pump, which is more efficient than gas or electric. Some landlords charge $25 or more a day to heat their pools for guests.

and rarely snows.

But in the snowy northern states, a garage is an attractive feature for people renting homes. It protects their cars from the elements and offers extra storage for their belongings.

If you find a house with a carport, you might be able to convert it into a garage. Doing that also could boost the value of your property to renters and future buyers.

Yard Size

A condo is not expected to have a large yard. Often all you get is a small balcony or patio. A rental home does not have to have a large yard. In fact, the bigger the yard, the more maintenance for you.

However, families with children often rent a house because an apartment is too confining. So whether long- or short-term, I would never purchase a rental home unless it had a decent-sized backyard. Dogs also appreciate a backyard.

Property Taxes

Property taxes can be a big expense in many areas of the country, even for lower-priced homes. And taxes can vary substantially across different communities in a metropolitan area.

Arizona property taxes are up to 50 percent lower than taxes in many other areas of the country. But they vary considerably across communities in Arizona.

When I bought my house in Phoenix a decade ago, I looked at areas in both Phoenix and Glendale, which is on the west side of the metropolitan area. I compared similar homes and found that property taxes in Glendale were 20 percent higher than similar homes in Phoenix.

Why?

After a little online research, I discovered that the city of Glendale carries most of the debt on construction of the stadium where the Arizona Cardinals have played football since 2006.

"Though Glendale only has 240,000 residents, state and local taxpayers picked up $312 million of the stadium's $455 million cost," writes Jared Meyer, a senior research fellow at the Foundation for Government Accountability. "More than 40 percent of the city's debt comes from its sports complexes."[112]

I decided to buy in Phoenix.

The lesson here is to pay attention to the little details when it comes to buying a property. Look at the buying and tax history of a property closely. And who is selling it. Flippers often overprice a property. You can usually spot this when you see a big discrepancy between the last sale price just a month or so before and the current price. Check the prices of similar properties nearby to confirm this. This information is easily accessible through Zillow when you click on a property.

Rental Rates in the Area

In addition to providing estimated property values for properties, Zillow estimates the monthly rental rates for most homes and condos. Check the amount on the property you intend to purchase. Check other homes in the area. And check Apartments.com or another rental site to see how much apartments are going for in the area.

You can add or subtract amounts from your proposed rental rate if your property has more amenities than a comparable property. For

---

[112]Jared Meyer, "NFL's Real '12th Man' Is the Taxpayer," Manhattan Institute (January 14, 2016; article originally appeared in *Reason*), retrieved 1/3/24 from <https://manhattan.institute/article/nfls-real-12th-man-is-the-taxpayer-2>.

example, my home has a big in-ground heated swimming pool. If I leased it long-term, I estimate I could get $200 or more extra per month. I would hire a company to maintain the pool. I wouldn't leave it up to the tenants, because most do not have the knowledge to care for a pool.

Cash Flow and Profit

The final and most important criteria for selecting a rental property are to estimate how much cash flow and profit you can turn on the property. These are two separate matters. Cash flow shows whether you are able to cover all bills on a rental property. The goal is to have some left over to pay yourself at least a small salary.

The question of profit includes the matter of cash flow but also shows how much money your property will make in the long run from appreciation, principal payments, and depreciation. If your cash flow is adequate but the appreciation rate is small, your property will not produce a lot of profits in the long run. You'll pay the bills but your path to wealth could take a long time.

The next chapter focuses on cash flow. I use my Sun City property as an example. Chapter 15 focuses on profit. I will present a fairly detailed model for calculating profit on your proposed rental.

How to Calculate Cash Flow

The terms cash flow and profit are sometimes used interchangeably. If you have a positive cash flow, that generally means your rental property is turning a profit. Your income exceeds your expenses.

However, the reverse is not necessarily true.

Your property can post a negative cash flow but still make a profit, at least in the long haul. That's because appreciation is a major source of income on a rental property, and appreciation profits cannot be accessed until the property is sold or tapped through an equity loan.

So you can run a negative cash flow on a property but still make money on it when you sell it. As long as you have extra cash, you can continue paying the bills. But if you don't have extra cash, then you should avoid buying a property that won't generate a positive cash flow.

Of course, the ideal property generates a positive cash flow as well as a healthy amount of appreciation. In this chapter, I'll show you how to calculate cash flow using my Sun City property as an example. I purchased it in 2019 and sold it in 2021.

Finding the Cash Flow Tipping Point

To estimate cash flow, you need to first find out how much rent you can charge on your proposed rental property. In 2019, the rental rates in

Sun City for a 2-bedroom, 2-bath home or condo were about $1,300 a month. That is a *tipping point*. If the mortgage and other expenses on a property exceed that amount, I would incur a negative cash flow.

Now I need to make a list of my expenses. They include the mortgage payment, taxes, insurance, fees, maintenance, and utilities.

Estimating Mortgage Payments

The mortgage payment is likely the biggest bill you'll have to pay on a rental property. I used an online mortgage calculator to estimate my rate before I purchased. I found it at *amortization-calc.com/mortgage-calculator*. There are many other mortgage calculators out there.

The site requested four pieces information: (1) home price, (2) down payment, (3) loan term (number of years), and (4) interest rate. The asking price was $140,000. I financed the whole thing because I used my Phoenix house as collateral. Most buyers without equity in a property would put 25 percent down to purchase a rental property.

So the home price was $140,000 (I actually paid $139,000 but used the extra $1,000 to pay closing costs). The down payment was zero. The loan term was 30 years. My interest rate was 4.5 percent. To estimate your interest rates (if you don't have one from your lending institution already), go to this government website managed by the Federal Reserve, which provides the current national average mortgage rate (*https://fred.stlouisfed.org/series/MORTGAGE30US*).

Your actual rate will vary depending upon your credit rating, how much you put down, and how many *mortgage points* you buy. Points (also called loan origination fees) are paid directly to the lender at closing to obtain a reduced interest rate. When you "*buy down the rate*," you basically pay interest on the loan in advance. One point costs about 1 percent of your loan amount, which comes out to $1,000 for every $100,000.

In general, I recommend that you don't pay points, because they decrease your leverage. Points, by the way, must be depreciated (not deducted from your taxes) over the length of the loan (usually 30 years), because the law doesn't allow prepayment of interest in a single year.[113]

For me, the bottom line was that I would have an estimated monthly payment of $709, with $525 initially going to pay interest and $184 to principal. My estimated costs were less than the mortgage payment.

Estimating Other Costs

1. *Taxes.* In Arizona, the law prohibits the government from raising property taxes by more than 5 percent per year. Over time, though, properties tend to increase in value at a faster pace. So when the property is sold, the property valuation and, thus, taxes are recalculated based in part on the new sale price.

   The Zillow estimate of taxes may under report the final tax amount I would owe. So I did a search of 2-bedroom homes in Sun City that recently sold for exactly $140,000 (about 30 homes popped up) and I randomly selected seven and clicked on the links to find the most recent tax bills on those homes: ($631, $548, $513, $503, $487, $457 and $327). Adding those amounts and dividing by seven gave me an average yearly rate of $495, or $41 a month.

2. *Insurance.* My insurance company gave me an estimate of $520 for a landlord policy on a condominium. This included $100,000/$300,000 coverage, which means $100,000 per person for bodily injuries sustained in one incident and topping out at a maximum payout of $300,000 for all claims.

---

[113]The law is more complicated when the amount of points paid exceeds $7,500. See IRS Form 4562, *Depreciation and Amortization.* There are also limitations on interest deductions by landlords earning $25 million or more. (Wouldn't that be a nice problem to have?)

The policy also covered the costs of repairing or rebuilding the condo if it was damaged or destroyed. Condominium owners pay a lot less for insurance than they would for a single family detached home, because the outside walls and roof are usually insured by the Homeowners Association. HOA fees pay this cost. My monthly insurance cost was $42.

3. *Advertising.* I included a small amount, $25 a year, to cover the costs of buying a yard sign to advertise the rental property ($2 a month). Landlords can advertise for free their long-term rental units on Zillow, which also posts your listing on Trulia and HotPads. But you have the option of purchasing some of their management tools, such as tenant screening and rent payment systems. Your tenants also can sign leases and make payments through the site, which is easy to use.[114]

5. *Recreation Fee.* The community of Sun City charges homeowners a $496 yearly recreation fee on all properties. This came out to about $41 a month. This fee helps maintain the seven recreational facilities, golf courses, swimming pools, and arts, crafts, and hobbies centers.

6. *Gas/Electric Utilities.* Tenants normally pay for the gas and electricity on a long-term rental property. But when the home is vacant (average one month a year), I will have to pay. I estimated the power bills would be about $100 a year, or about $8 a month.

7. *HOA Fees.* HOA fees were $190 a month, which covered water/sewer/trash and outside maintenance, including landscaping. Most landlords pay the water, sewer, and trash services, because if a tenant fails to pay the services could be turned off. Imagine what would happen if the toilets weren't flushed. In Sun City, the average cost of these services was $68 month.

---

[114]The rental management page at Zillow.com can be found at this link: <https://www.zillow.com/rental-manager/?itc=ltr_zw_cr_zrn-splitter_btn_list-properties>.

8. *Routine Maintenance/Repairs/Reserve Fund.* Maintenance costs are difficult to predict. But real estate experts say you should put aside about 1% of the total value of the property each year.[115] I didn't need that much, because I had no outside maintenance fees or landscaping fees. So I estimated $85 for inside maintenance and reserve fund.

Cash Flow Estimate on My Sun City Condo

So the estimated monthly expenses on my Sun City Condo were as follows: (1) mortgage, $709; (2) taxes, $41; (3) insurance, $42; (4) advertising, $2; (5) recreation fee, $41; (6) gas/electric (when unit is unoccupied), $11; (7) HOA fees, which included water/sewer/trash, $190; and (8) routine maintenance, repair, and reserve fund, $85.

The total comes out to $1,121, which subtracted from a monthly rent of $1,300 left a positive cash flow of $179 a month, or $2,148 a year. Not much, but enough cushion should the short-term rental plan go belly-up. So I decided to make an offer. But before doing that, I want to show you how to estimate your profits for at least 10 years into the future. This information will enhance your ability to make a good buying decision.

---

[115]Leonard Baron, "Investing 101: Estimating Rental Property Expenses," Zillow (not dated), retrieved 1/3/24 from <https://www.zillow.com/learn/investing-101-estimating-rental-property-expenses>.

How to Estimate Profits on Your Rental

There's nothing wrong with the method I used in the last chapter to estimate cash flow before purchasing my condo in Sun City.

You need cash flow to pay the bills.

However, that method can't tell me the exact profit I would earn on my property now or into the future, because it only included rental income. It didn't include three other sources of income: appreciation, equity from principal payments, and depreciation.

Estimating profits on rental property is no exact science.

Many factors that affect income and expenses are changing. Inflation, for example, varies by type of expense or source of income. Landlord insurance rates have been rising faster than other kinds of expenses, but rental rate increases have slowed considerably.

This chapter shows you how to estimate profits on your proposed or existing property for the first year.

You can easily extend these profit estimates into future years by making historically grounded assumptions about inflationary costs on sources of income as well as expenditures. I do this in the Appendix for my Phoenix rental home and for a hypothetical $300,000 rental home with a $75,000 down payment and $14,000 down payment.

The goal is to reduce your risk in terms of deciding whether to buy a property.

Estimating Sources of Income

Every market and rental property is different, so to estimate profits for your potential rental, you'll need to gather information about expected income and expenses. As noted previously in this book, I identify four major sources of income and five major sources of expenses. I'll start with income.

A1 – Estimating Rental Income

How much rent can you charge if you lease the rental property for one full year?

Don't worry about short-term rental rates right now.

If you can't turn a profit on a long-term lease, don't buy it, because if another pandemic occurs or your property isn't suitable for the short-term rental market, you could lose your shirt. There are no guarantees a short-term rental property will succeed even in popular tourist destinations, like Phoenix. I know this because I occasionally compare my short-term rental to others on Vrbo and Airbnb, and I often discover that many of them have very few bookings. Often the owner is charging too much. There's been a lot of hype about getting rich through short-term rentals. Ignore that. Instead, you need to be sure you can turn a profit on a long-term lease before buying a property. That's your backup plan.

There are several ways to estimate how much rent you can charge on a property. The easiest, as I mentioned in the last chapter, is to go to Zillow.com, which provides the appraised value of your target property as well as long-term rental rates. Its algorithms scan sales data of homes in your area to produce these estimates. Although the estimates are not always precise, I have been following them for more than two decades and they are generally reliable, sometimes underestimating the values of homes and rental rates (better than overestimating).

In my case, Zillow estimated that I could rent my Phoenix home for $2,300 a month on a long-term lease. That was enough to cover my DSCR mortgage loan, excluding taxes and insurance. I had additional income to cover these non-mortgage expenses, so if my short-term rental strategy failed, I knew I could convert my home into a long-term rental and it would do well. I also knew that I could add $200 more to the rent because I had a large swimming pool in the backyard. Some renters are willing to pay extra for that amenity, especially in sunny Phoenix. So if I were to rent my house long-term, I could get $2,500 and perhaps even a wee bit more.

There are other ways to estimate rent.

You can look at the rates of nearby apartment complexes that are similar to your property in terms of number of bedrooms and bathrooms and in terms of square footage. Because you're offering a house with a backyard, and perhaps a garage and other amenities, you can charge a little more.

You can also look at Zillow and other websites that offer information on rental homes and condominiums in the neighborhood where your rental is located. Just be realistic in terms of your rental income estimate. Better to go low than high.

Enter your estimate of long-term annual rental income in row A1 of Table 15.1 on the next page.

A2 – Estimating Appreciation

Zillow also gives you estimates of how much a property has changed in value over the last month. Of course, there are no guarantees the change will be repeated in the coming months. But Zillow also shows you how property values have changed over the past 10 years, and you

Table 15.1

Estimating Profits for a Long-Term Lease

(Enter Amounts Below to Calculate the Estimated Profit on Your Proposed Property)

Long-Term Annual Income	
A1. Rental Income	
A2. Appreciation	
A3. Principal (equity from)	
A4. Depreciation (savings from)	
A5. Other income	
SUBTOTAL A (INCOME)	
Expenses	
B1. Mortgage Payment (Interest & Principal)	
B2. Landlord Insurance	
B3. Property Taxes	
B4. Maintenance/repairs/landscaping/reserve fund	
B5. Utilities (water/sewer/trash)*	
B6. Other expenses (e.g., HOA fees)	
SUBSTOTAL B (EXPENSES)	
PROFIT (Subtotal B subtracted from Subtotal A)	

*Electricity/gas/Internet service, Cable TV typically paid by tenant on long-term lease.

can use that trend (if your property is that old) to predict future values.

Click on the "Zestimate history and details" tab. Using a ruler, draw a straight best-fitting line through all of the values and extend it into the future. That will give you a rough estimate of where the value will be in future years.

To provide a more precise estimate of future values, move the cursor on your mouse back to the oldest value (usually about 10 years ago). Record the date and amount. Take that value (we'll call that the "old value"), subtract it from the current (most recent) value ("new value"), and then divide by the old value. This will give you an estimate of the return on investment (ROI).

Here's an example using my Phoenix condo. Its value 10 years ago was $74,000. The current value is $256,000. So the overall gain, or return on investment, is 246 percent [($256,000 – $74,000) ÷ $74,000].

If you divide by 10, the average gain each year is 24.6 percent. But that figure fails to take into account the compounding of interest over time. This is called the annualized gain (see Text Box 2.2), which enables you to predict future gains with more accuracy.

To calculate the annualized gain, use a compound interest calculator.[116] Begin by entering the initial value of the property ($74,000) and the number of years (10), and then adjust the interest rate level until you arrive at a figure close to $256,000. In this case, the average annualized gain is about 13 percent. So you can expect your property grow in value about 13 percent each year.

When you estimate appreciation, it is generally wise to err on the conservative side. So I rounded down to 10 percent, which would generate $25,600 in appreciation in the first year, and $28,160 in the second year, etc. In 10 years, the $256,000 property would have an estimated worth of $664,000.[117] By the way, my rental home in Phoenix increased in value at an annualized rate of 11 percent each year during

---

[116]I recommend the compound interest calculator at <https://www.investor.gov/financial-tools-calculators/calculators/compound-interest-calculator>. There is a formula for calculating the annualized gain, but it's too difficult and complicated to do it by hand.

[117]Appreciation in all three appendices in the back of this book is compounded.

the past 10 years. This was less than the Phoenix condominium because there is more demand for lower-priced properties, which drives the price up.

The upshot is that income from appreciation will grow very quickly on these properties. That's not too surprising, because demand for housing in Phoenix is far greater than the supply. Fifty thousand people are moving here each year, partly because of the warm weather and partly because of jobs. Many high-tech firms are building facilities here. And contrary to national news stories, Phoenix is not running out of water. It has enough water to supply the area for another one hundred years.[118]

Enter your estimated appreciation in row A2 of Table 15.1.

A3 – Estimating Principal (Equity) Payments

The third source of income for a rental property is equity from principal payments. The rental income you earn from the property will pay the monthly mortgage bill. The principal part of that payment is money in your pocket. You will get that back when you sell or borrow on the equity in the property.

As you probably know, in the early years most of the mortgage payment goes to pay the interest and only a small amount is put toward paying off the principal, which was the amount you borrowed to buy the property. Your monthly mortgage statement will show you how much of the payment went to interest and how much to principal.

The amount that goes to principal is like putting money in the bank. When you pay off all of the principal, you own the property free and

---

[118]Sarah Porter and Kathryn Sorensen, "Phoenix Is in No Danger of Running Out of Water," *Wall Street Journal* (October 6, 2023), retrieved 12/22/23 from <https://www.wsj.com/articles/phoenix-is-in-no-danger-of-running-out-of-water-9f0d3b1e>.

clear. Meanwhile, if you sell the property before then, you will owe less than the original amount borrowed, because you've made payments toward the principal. This equity, in other words, is a form of income.

If you look at Appendix 1, you can see the amount of principal that I paid or will pay in the next 10 years on my rental home. Note that it is not a large sum of money, because most of the payment goes to interest in the early years. But during the last 10 years of a 30-year loan (not shown in the table), a substantial amount of the mortgage payment goes to paying down the principal.

Enter your estimated equity from principal in row A3 of Table 15.1.

A4 – Estimating Income from Depreciation

The fourth and last major source of income comes from depreciation, although the savings from this can be difficult to calculate because it depends in part on the total income you make during the year.

The IRS treats depreciation as an expense. But because it typically reduces a tax bill, most landlords think of it as a source of income (less taxes to pay). It's a bit complicated, so let me illustrate using the $300,000 rental property shown in Table 4.1 and Appendix 2.

As I've noted before, a home is typically depreciated in 27.5 years. If you paid $300,000 for the home and the land is worth $60,000 (20% of the total price), you can depreciate $240,000 of the total from your income over 27.5 years. So each year you deduct 1/27.5 (or 3.64%), which comes to about $8,727 each year (see row G in Table 2.1 or Column F in Appendix 2).

If your 2023 income was between $44,726 and $95,375 in 2023, you typically saved about $1,920 on your tax bill (in Table 4.1, subtract Line H from Line F, $5,068 – $3,148).

If you made less than $44,726, you probably didn't get much of a tax break on depreciation, because your income was too low. However, the undeducted amount can be carried over into future years until you use it or sell your property, at which time the entire sum can be deducted before you pay taxes.

One other cautionary note.

As you depreciate your property, you save on taxes. But when you sell the property, the IRS will assess a depreciation recapture tax of 25 percent on the depreciation you took, and you'll have to pay capital gains taxes on the appreciation as well.

So the question of whether depreciation is a wash or a source of income is up to you. But there are ways to eliminate this tax (which means it would be a source of income) and capital gains taxes. I'll tackle these issues in Chapters 21 and 22.

In short, if you consider depreciation to be a source of income, enter your expected savings on line A4 in Table 15.1.

Estimating Sources of Expenses

B1 – Estimating the Mortgage Payment

The biggest expense on a rental property is usually the mortgage payment. Although you may be able to pay cash for a property, to maximize your assets you should consider putting down the least amount of money on a property you can. As I noted in Chapter 2, leveraging other people's money is how many real estate moguls became moguls.

Estimating the cost of a mortgage is easy if you use an online mortgage calculator.[119] Mortgage calculators will ask you to input the purchase price, down payment, interest rate, term of loan, and start date. They automatically generate the loan amount and monthly payments

---

[119]I like the one at <https://www.mortgagecalculator.org>, because it has a summary graphic at top and you can create a variety of amortization tables to meet your needs.

after subtracting the down payment from the purchase price. The amortization tables also show you how much the entire loan will cost and how much of your payment is going to interest and principal over the life of the loan.

Some of the calculators also ask you to include property taxes and landlord insurance, but you don't have enter them. These two items are usually included in the monthly mortgage payment because the lending institution, which holds partial ownership of the home, wants to protect its interests. If you fail to pay the insurance and your rental burned down, the lending institution could lose its investment, especially if you don't have the cash to pay the balance on the loan.

Part of your mortgage payment will be set aside in an *escrow account*[120] to pay the insurance and taxes. These amounts are usually distributed once or twice a year to the billing entities.

Table 15.2 provides a summary of the mortgage costs for a $300,000 rental home or condominium. The results for two types of loans are presented: (1) a conventional loan, which usually requires a 25 percent down payment for a rental property to avoid paying mortgage insurance, and (2) a Federal Housing Authority (FHA) loan, which usually has lower down payments and interest rates for qualifying borrowers.

However, FHA borrowers typically will have to pay a *mortgage insurance premium* (MIP) and a *property mortgage insurance* (PMI) fee, both of which guarantee payment to lenders or the loan program if a borrower defaults. Both of these fees can add substantial amounts to the cost of a loan, depending upon the size of the loan, down payment, and credit-worthiness of the borrower. Write-in the estimate for you mortgage payment on line B1 in Table 15.1.

---

[120]Escrow is a legal arrangement in which a third party temporarily holds money until a purchase agreement has been completed or a demand for payment on insurance or property taxes is made. The escrow company then releases the funds to the creditor.

Table 15.2

Mortgage Costs for a $300,000 Rental Home or Condo

Mortgage Inputs	Conventional Loan 25% Down	FHA or VA Loan 3.5% Down	Your Mortgage Loan
Purchase Price	$300,000	$300,000	
Down Payment	$75,000	$10,500	
Loan Amount	$225,000	$289,500	
Interest Rate	7%	7%	
Loan Term	30 Years	30 Years	
Start Date	January 2024	January 2024	
Mortg Insurance Prem (MIP)*	NA	1.75%	
Prop Mortg Insurance (PMI)	NA	0.58–1.86%	
Monthly HOA Fee	NA	NA	
Mortgage Payments			
Total First Year	$17,963	$23,113	
Payment w/o PMI	$1,863	$2,293	
With PMI Payment	NA	$2,413	
One-Time Expenses			
Closing Costs**	$12,000	$12,000	
Mortg Ins Prem (MIP)	NA	$5,066	

*MIP is a one-time fee at closing. See One-Time Expenses below for amount.
**Buyer closing costs for an average $300,000 home in the United States are between 2% and 6%, according to Nerdwallet. I used 4% to calculate the costs shown in the table. For more info, see <https://www.nerdwallet.com/article/ mortgages/closing-costs-mortgage-fees-explained>.

B2 – Estimating Landlord Insurance

There are two types of insurance when it comes to rental properties. The first is renters insurance, which covers losses from the renter, not the landlord. Many landlords require renters to obtain renters insurance for their personal belongings because landlord policies do not cover them. So if a fire occurs and destroys the renter's personal possessions in the rental unit, they will only be able to be compensated for the loss if they have renters insurance.[121]

The second type of insurance is landlord insurance. That's the one you will purchase. Landlord insurance is usually about 25 percent more expensive than homeowners insurance. There's more risk with tenants, who typically do not treat the property with the same respect as a homeowner.

Be sure to inform your insurance company about whether you are leasing your property on a short-term versus long-term basis. The former can typically cost a bit more. You don't want to run the risk of your insurance company refusing to pay a claim because it didn't know it was a short-term rental.

The cost of insurance will depend on many factors, including the community or neighborhood in which your property is located, the value of your home, the amount of coverage you need, your deductible amount, and sometimes your creditworthiness.

In Phoenix, the policy for my home with a $5,000 deductible was $1,300 a year. But the national average for a $300,000 rental home appears to be closer to $2,000.[122]

---

[121]There are some exceptions to this rule. If the landlord is negligent, the tenant may obtain compensation. Be sure your units comply with housing and safety regulations.

[122]Ashley Kilroy, "What Is Landlord Insurance? What Does It Cover?" *Forbes Advisor* (October 27, 2023), retrieved 11/7/23 from <https://www.forbes.com/advisor/homeowners-insurance/landlord-insurance>.

To obtain an estimate of landlord insurance, contact a couple of companies and they will give you quotes. Enter the amount on line B2 in Table 15.1.

B3 – Estimating Property Taxes

The average property tax bill for a $300,000 home in the United States is $3,000 a year. But this amount can vary considerably from state to state and city to city. For a big city, Phoenix has some of the lowest property taxes in the country. For my $460,000 home, they were $1,763 in 2023.

The governmental agencies that collect and disseminate tax information vary from place to place. You can typically obtain the tax bill from the county assessor's office and/or the county treasurer. This information is often available online. Zillow also usually posts the property tax bill.

Enter the amount on line B3 in Table 15.1.

B4 – Estimating Maintenance/Reserve Fund

If you already own a house, you may have a good idea of how much you spend on maintenance, repairs, and landscaping.

I would just add that if you decide to lease your home through Airbnb or Vrbo, be aware that these costs likely will be higher. Guests do not take care of a home like you do.

They don't own it.

That said, whenever guests have damaged something in my home (such as a screen door), they have always reimbursed me. Both Airbnb and Vrbo have plans for reimbursing you for damages (more on that in Chapter 18).

If you don't own a property yet, one of three options are often used to estimate maintenance costs on a rental property[123]:

- The *50% Rule* recommends you set aside half of your rental income each month for expenses on your property. I don't recommend this approach, because taxes and insurance vary substantially and if you have a mortgage, you likely will be paying those in your monthly mortgage.

- The *1% Rule* assumes that maintenance will cost about 1 percent of the property value per year. So, if your property is valued at $300,000, then maintenance will cost about $3,000, or about $250 a month.

- The *Square Footage Rule* says you should set aside $1 per square foot for annual maintenance costs. So a 2,000-square-foot rental will need $2,000 in maintenance costs per year, or about $167 a month. This rule tends to be less conservative than the 1 percent rule.

I also recommend you set up a reserve or contingency account to cover unexpected major costs, such as a breakdown in a refrigerator or an air conditioning unit.

To estimate your maintenance costs on a proposed rental property, I recommendation you use both the 1% Rule and the Square Footage Rule and then select the one that sets aside the most money. I used the 1 percent rule on my 2,000-square-foot house and then added another $400 more for pool maintenance and supplies (costs have risen substantially since COVID). During my first year, I also had an unexpected $700 repair for a broken element.

Enter your estimated maintenance/repair plus reserve fund costs in line B4 in Table 15.1.

---

[123]Homee Team, "Rental Property Maintenance Expenses: How to Estimate Operating Costs," Homee.com (March 09, 2020), retrieved 11/8/23 from <https://www.homee.com/blog/rental-property-maintenance-expenses>.

B5 – Utilities (electricity/natural gas/water/sewer/trash)

Electricity and natural gas are often one of the biggest expenses on a rental property aside from the mortgage.

In 2023, the average monthly residential electricity bill in the United States was $143.[124] The average natural gas bill was $63.[125] Electricity prices increased 26 percent from 2000 to 2023.[126] Natural gas prices are roughly unchanged, but there were price spikes in 2005, 2008, and 2022.[127]

If you own your own property, your energy bills will enable you to make fairly accurate estimates of the cost. But if you lease your property on a long-term contract, you typically won't have to enter them into Table 15.1, because these costs are usually borne by the tenants. With short-term contracts, you'll have take these costs into account.

Also note that short-term guests will typically put the thermostat at a level that is comfortable to them. You'll likely find that the bills when guests are staying there are higher than your bills if you actively conserve energy to keep your costs down.

The costs of water, sewer, and trash are usually borne by the landlord. Many landlords prefer to pay these bills because they don't want these utilities shut off if the tenant doesn't pay the bill.

These costs typically are covered by rent.

---

[124]Save on Energy Team, "Electricity Bill Report: November 2023," SaveOnEnergy.com (November 3, 2023), retrieved November 11, 2023, from <https://www.saveonenergy.com/resources/electricity-bills-by-state>.

[125]Lauren Schwahn, "How Much Is the Average Gas Bill, and How Can I Lower Mine?" Nerdwallet (August 11, 2023), retrieved November 8, 2023 from <https://www.nerdwallet.com/article/finance/gas-bill>.

[126]"Average retail electricity prices in the United States in selected years from 1990 to 2022 (in U.S. cents per kilowatt-hour)," Statista (2023), retrieved 11/8/23 from <https://www.statista.com/statistics/183700/us-average-retail-electricity-price-since-1990>.

[127]"Natural Gas: Historical Data," Trading Economics (November 8, 2023), retrieved 11/8/23 from <https://tradingeconomics.com/commodity/natural-gas>.

The rates for these services vary considerably depending on market. For example, my water/trash/sewer bill in Arizona is about $60 a month. In Spokane, Washington, however, I was paying $300 for water every other month in the summer and $150 on the opposite months and $100 for trash collection every month.

Add your costs for utilities on line B5 in Table 15.1.

Calculating Your Estimated Profits

In Chapter 3, I presented the estimated annual profits for a short-term $300,000 rental property, which was $41,049 — a figure that includes $15,000 for estimated appreciation and $3,012 for equity from principal payments and depreciation. This means that the property is generating a cash flow of $23,037 above and beyond all expenses ($41,049 – $15,000 – $3,012). This is a comfortable margin that enables you to take home some profits and also cover unexpected major bills (see Appendix 2 for more details).

The property also turns a $17,775 profit when leased long-term. But cash-flow drops to $489 when appreciation and equity from principal are excluded (see Appendix 2, column B1; note that there is no income from depreciation because the estimates assume the landlord doesn't have any other earned income). They key point here is that if you don't have extra cash or income, you may not want to buy the property.

So add up the income and expenses in Table 15.1 for your property and subtract the expenses from the income.

How did it come out?

If there is no positive cash, consider looking for a less expensive property or wait until interest rates drop. If the positive cash flow is under $400 a month, be cautious. Although the appreciated value of your property will grow quickly under normal conditions, if you don't have discretionary income to cover unexpected expenses, you could have a shortfall. If the cash flow is $500 or more a month, then, only speaking for myself, I would proceed. Until the mortgage is paid off, the big money from rental real estate comes from appreciation over time.[128] But you will make the final decision.

---

[128]If your mortgage is paid off, then rental income will generate a lot of cash flow. But to maximize leverage, you shouldn't pay off a mortgage. You should draw the equity and purchase another property. This is the fastest path to wealth in real estate.

Closing the Real Estate Deal

If you believe you can turn a decent profit (cash flow and appreciation) on a rental property and there are no other red flags, make an offer.

Some investors push the idea that getting a good deal depends on knowing the motivations of the seller and your ability to negotiate.

Perhaps.

But don't be consumed with trying to figure out how to outwit the seller. Predicate your offer on a price that ensures you can turn a profit. That's the key. If the seller doesn't accept, look for another property. Don't get too wrapped up in any single property.

The Purchase Agreement

Your real estate agent will draft a *purchase agreement* to present to the seller and/or her agent.[129] Although it looks complicated, it's not. The first part identifies the location of the property and the legal description. There are 10 or so more elements, depending upon the property and the needs of the seller and buyer.

---

[129]An example of a real estate purchase agreement can be found at this Utah government website: <https://realestate.utah.gov/wp-content/uploads/2023/03/purchase-contract.pdf>.

1. *Property Address and What's Included.* Of course, one of the first items on the purchase agreement is the address of the property being sold, along with the local or state tax identification number. Typically everything on the property is transferred in the sale, but some items may be specifically excluded.

2. *Purchase Price.* Along with the price, this section of the contract typically includes information about the *earnest money deposit*, which shows that you are serious about buying the property. If you back out of the deal, you'll lose this money. Typically the earnest deposit is 1 to 2 percent of the purchase price, but a buyer who puts down more will be in a preferential position should another offer of near equal value be on the table. Most buyers prefer cash, because the deal closes quickly and some unforeseen event, like buyers not qualifying for a loan, doesn't torpedo the deal.

3. *Settlement and Closing.* This item stipulates when the seller will turn over possession of the property, and it's usually when the sale is recorded.

4. *Prorations/Assessments/Taxes and Rents.* This items states that taxes, rents, and/or HOA fees will be prorated at the time of the sale.

5. *Title and Title Insurance.* The seller will transfer a legally clear general warranty deed to the buyer. In other words, the seller is guaranteeing that they are the rightful property owner and have a legal right to transfer title. The seller also agrees to pay for title insurance to cover any deed transfer problems should they arise.

6. *Risk of Loss.* Until the sale, the seller assumes responsibility for all losses or damage to the property.

7. *Buyer's Conditions.* The buyer has an obligation to use due diligence

by inspecting the property before the closing, and the seller agrees to cooperate. If the buyer fails to identify a problem before the sale is consummated (see checklist in Text Box 15.1), the buyer is tough out of luck.

8. *General Conditions.* Both parties agree the contract is binding on heirs and representatives. This protects the parties in case one of them dies or is unable to close the deal.

9. *Contingency or Special Conditions.* The parties can add special conditions or contingencies to the contract. A *contingency clause* gives the seller or buyer a right to back out if a condition is not met. Perhaps the most common contingency for buyers is making the sale contingent on a professional inspection. If the inspector finds major problems, such as mold, the buyer can back out without losing the earnest money.

As the buyer, you accept the asking price or offer a lower price and sign the contract. Your agent will deliver it to the seller's agent. If the seller doesn't like the offer, the seller can make a counter-offer within a specified short period of time (a day or two). Negotiations continue until both parties accept the agreement or one "walks away."

Due Diligence

When the agreement is signed by both parties, then *due diligence* begins — a period of time (usually several days to a week) during which you and your home inspector investigate the property's physical condition. If any problems are found (see Text Box 16.1), you can ask the seller to correct them or provide financial compensation, in which case you will take responsibility for fixing them.

When these issues are finalized, a closing date is set up, at which time both parties sign all of the contracts and agreements to consummate

Text Box 16.1
Due Diligence Checklist

Exterior Inspection

- Roof problems, including signs of leaks
- The condition of heating, ventilation, and cooling systems
- Electrical wiring that is not in compliance with current codes
- The condition of the exterior paint and trim
- The condition of the driveways and parking lots
- Landscaping problems: sprinkler system breaks, trees that need trimming, root growth that is cracking sidewalks/foundations
- Insect/pest problems, such as termites and cockroaches

Interior Inspection

- Holes in walls, damage to countertops and cabinets
- Are the plumbing and electrical working? Bad outlets?
- Are the ceilings sagging? Are there water stains on the ceilings?
- Condition of appliances and other items
- Major water, fire, or resident damage
- Bug and pest problems

Safety Inspection

- Fire code violations
- Have any remodels, additions, pools, been added without required permits?
- Environmental problems: asbestos, mold, lead paint, radon gas
- Zoning violations or encroachment onto another property

the deal. Today this is often done online. No physical meeting is necessary. In fact, buyers and sellers typically never meet each other in person.

Property Insurance

At the closing, you'll need an insurance policy to protect your investment, should it be damaged by fire or storm or someone is injured on your property. Landlords are sued more often than any other type of business entity.

If no guest or tenant is occupying the property, your insurance company will issue a *vacate home policy* until the unit is rented. A typical policy covers losses to the physical property and losses from people who are injured, whether tenants or visitors. A typical policy also covers damages from fire, explosion, lightning, smoke, riot, hailstorm, wind, and sprinkler/water pipe leakage. But damage caused by earthquakes and floods usually is not covered. You'll have to pay extra to get these events covered, but if the property is in an area that floods occasionally, the extra cost may help you sleep at night.

Insurance policies can cover actual cash value or replacement cost. The former means replacement or repair of the damaged property less depreciation. The latter is more costly but often the best choice, because it means the full value of the property is covered.

Part VI
How to Manage a Property

Five Rules of Property Management

W hat's the biggest reason new landlords quit the business?

Bad tenants. Tenants who don't pay their rent. Tenants who destroy the property. Tenants who don't respect other tenants' rights or your rights as a property owner.

And what's the biggest reason landlords have bad tenants?

Landlords who don't manage their property well.

And why do some landlords fail to manage their properties well?

Because many of them buy properties that attract bad tenants.

So, the first rule of property management is this: (1) buy a property in a good market. The other four rules are (2) obey laws and ordinances, (3) always do background checks on tenants,[130] (4) use a legally valid lease agreement, and (5) treat tenants with respect but be unwavering.

1. Buy in a Good Market

If you buy a cheap house in a crime-ridden area of town, no matter what you do as a landlord, you will have trouble filling that unit with

---

[130]By the way, if your property is a short-term rental, you typically don't have to follow Rule #3. Airbnb and Vrbo collect the rental fees in advance (so you always get paid). They also block tenants who have damaged homes and failed to follow their rules and the landlord's rules.

quality tenants. People who are responsible don't like to live in areas where other people are not. You want responsible people in your rental properties.

As noted above, good markets attract good tenants, although a few bad ones slip through occasionally. But bad markets attract mostly bad tenants, and bad markets also are bad for your bottom line. The properties in them don't appreciate in value as quickly as properties in good areas.

So selecting a rental property in a good market is half the battle when it comes to obtaining good tenants. Here are four more rules.

2. Obey Laws and Ordinances

Tenant/landlord rules and laws apply not just to the tenant but to you, too. If you fail to follow the law, a court can hold you liable. Here are some of the things you must do as a landlord.

- *You must provide a safe and clean living unit.* This is required under all state and local laws and ordinances.

- *Whenever you need to enter the unit,* except in cases of emergencies, *you must give the tenant or guest advance notice.* Consult the laws in your state to determine how much advance notice you must give.

- *You must maintain your property.* After taking possession of your property, fix the things listed on the home inspection report as well as your inspection, especially those that pose a safety or health problem. This is very important. You can be held liable, for example, if a fire occurs, someone is injured, and you didn't repair a smoke detector.

  If your unit is occupied, some tenants might be irritated, but most will appreciate your efforts. When you take care of your property, you are taking care of them. This is also an opportunity for you to get to know your tenants, who can also draw attention to other problems that you and the inspector failed to detect.

One of the most important things you need to do is replace the batteries in smoke and carbon monoxide detectors. Never assume your residents will do this, even if the lease says it's their responsibility. Some laws require detectors to be electronically linked together so that when one goes off the others do as well. Even if the law doesn't require it, I always put fire extinguishers in my properties.

Pay attention to water and electrical problems, as an undetected leak in a pipe can produce unhealthy levels of mold in addition to expensive damages to drywall and framing. Broken outlets need to be fixed immediately. And respond promptly to tenants' maintenance complaints. This is one of the biggest reasons cited for not renewing a lease.

3. ALWAYS Screen Tenants

Notice that I capitalized ALWAYS. This includes people or friends you know who want to lease your property. I know that sounds unfriendly. But you may not know them as well as you think. And when irresponsible friends or acquaintances lease your unit, they may try to leverage their friendship to manipulate you, for example: "Can I give you the rent next week?"

Of course, the single biggest fear landlords face is that tenants or guests will fail to pay rent. The best way to eliminate this fear is to screen them. Every prospective tenant must complete a tenant background authorization application (see Figures 17.1a and 17.1b).[131]

The application includes information about the prospective tenant's finances, employment, address and others who will be living there. The

---

[131]Figures 17.1-1 and 17.1-2 were obtained 1/7/24 from <https://freeforms.com/wp-content/uploads/2021/01/Arizona-Residential-Rental-Application.pdf>.

Figure 17.1a

ARIZONA RENTAL APPLICATION

Property Address _____ Monthly Rent $ _____

Property Manager _____ Desired Move In Date_____

Current Information

Applicant Name	Co-Applicant Name
First: Middle: Last: Suffix:	First: Middle: Last: Suffix:
Social Security Number	Social Security Number
Date of Birth	Date of Birth
Drivers License Number & State	Drivers License Number & State
E-mail Address:	E-Mail Address:
Phone/Cell Phone	Phone/Cell Phone
Present Address:	Present Address:
City: State: Zip Code:	City: State: Zip Code:
Landlord	Landlord
Landlord Phone	Landlord Phone

<u>Other Occupants</u>
Name _____ Relationship _____ Date of Birth _____
Name _____ Relationship _____ Date of Birth _____
Name _____ Relationship _____ Date of Birth _____

<u>Pets</u>   Number _____
Type _____ Weight _____   Type _____ Weight _____
If dog what breed? _____   If dog what breed? _____

<u>Vehicle Information</u>
Make _____ Model _____ Year _____ State _____ License # _____
Make _____ Model _____ Year _____ State _____ License # _____
Make _____ Model _____ Year _____ State _____ License # _____

References

Nearest Relative (not living with you)	Nearest Relative (not living with you)
Name _____	Name _____
Address _____	Address _____
City _____ State _____ Zip _____	City _____ State _____ Zip _____
Phone _____	Phone _____

law gives you the authority to conduct a background check, including criminal history and credit reports, and you should inform your applicant that you are going to do this. Those who have criminal backgrounds will

Figure 17.1b

Have you Ever?

	Yes/No		Yes/No
PAID RENT LATE?		PAID RENT LATE?	
LEFT OWING RENT?		LEFT OWING RENT?	
BEEN EVICTED?		BEEN EVICTED?	
BROKE RENTAL AGREEMENT?		BROKE RENTAL AGREEMENT?	
LEFT PROPERTY DAMAGED?		LEFT PROPERTY DAMAGED?	
BEEN CONVICTED OF ANY CRIMINAL ACTIVITY?		BEEN CONVICTED OF ANY CRIMINAL ACTIVITY?	
BEEN CONVICTED OF A FELONY?		BEEN CONVICTED OF A FELONY?	
FILED FOR BANKRUPTCY?		FILED FOR BANKRUPTCY?	
DATE DISCHARGED: _____		DATE DISCHARGED: _____	

If you answered YES to any of the above, please explain:_____
_____
_____

Employment Information

Applicant	Co-Applicant
EMPLOYER _____	EMPLOYER _____
POSITION _____	POSITION _____
SUPERVISOR'S NAME _____	SUPERVISOR'S NAME _____
SUPERVISOR'S PHONE _____	SUPERVISOR'S PHONE _____
EMPLOYMENT DATE _____	EMPLOYMENT DATE _____
INCOME	INCOME
MONTHLY TAKE HOME $ _____	MONTHLY TAKE HOME $ _____
OTHER INCOME $ _____	OTHER INCOME $ _____
TOTAL MONTHLY INCOME $ _____	TOTAL MONTHLY INCOME $ _____

Credit Information

Bank _____	Bank _____
Branch _____	Branch _____
Account Type _____	Account Type _____

IMPORTANT INFORMATION – PLEASE READ BEFORE SIGNING
AUTHORIZATION

APPLICANT UNDERSTANDS THAT ONCE THE APPLICATION HAS BEEN APPROVED, AN EARNEST MONEY DEPOSIT IS REQUIRED FOR TAKING THE PROPERTY OFF THE MARKET. IT WILL BE DEPOSITED WITH THE LANDLORD/PROPERTY MANAGER. ONCE THE APPLICANT IS APPROVED BY THE **OWNER, OR OWNER'S AGENT**, AND A RENTAL AGREEMENT IS ENTERED INTO, THE EARNEST MONEY DEPOSIT WILL BE CREDITED TO THE REQUIRED SECURITY DEPOSIT. SAID DEPOSIT WILL BE **NON-REFUNDABLE** IF THE APPLICANT FAILS TO ENTER INTO THE RENTAL AGREEMENT OR FAILS TO TAKE OCCUPANCY ON THE DATE SPECIFIED. **CASHIER'S CHECK OR MONEY ORDER IS REQUIRED FOR PAYMENT OF THE DEPOSIT AND THE FIRST MONTH'S RENT.**

APPLICANT UNDERSTANDS THAT FAILURE TO SIGN THIS APPLICATION AND PROVIDE COMPLETE INFORMATION WILL CAUSE DELAYS IN PROCESSING AND MAY CAUSE THE APPLICATION TO BE REJECTED OR ANOTHER, COMPLETED APPLICATION TO BE ACCEPTED.

THE INFORMATION ON THIS APPLICATION IS TRUE AND CORRECT. I HEREBY AUTHORIZE THE LANDLORD/PROPERTY MANAGER TO INVESTIGATE THE INFORMATION SUPPLIED BY ME AND TO CONDUCT INQUIRES CONCERNING MY INCOME, FAMILY COMPOSITION, AND MODE OF LIVING, CREDIT AND CHARACTER FOR THE PURPOSE OF VERIFYING AND QUALIFYING FOR RESIDENCY. A FULL DISCLOSURE OF PERTINENT FACTS MAY BE MADE TO THE AGENT AND HOME OWNER. FALSIFYING INFORMATION ON THIS APPLICATION IS GROUNDS FOR DENIAL AND FORFEITURE OF DEPOSITS.

_____ Date _____   _____ Date _____
APPLICANT   CO-APPLICANT

often pull their application when they hear this, saving you the time and cost of conducting the background check.

To save time and money, I recommend you pay an outside company to conduct the criminal and credit background checks. A number of firms will do that, including TenantBackgroundSearch.com and MySmartMove.com. They charge $35 to $100 depending upon what you want, but this small fee can save you thousands of dollars if you have to evict.

The tenant usually pays the cost of the background check, but make sure your state law allows that. A nice gesture is to deduct the cost of the background check from the tenant's first month's rent.

In addition to a criminal and credit rating check, you should ensure the prospective tenant has a stable work history and has enough income to pay the rent. A general rule is that the cost of rent should not exceed 30 percent of the resident's total income or 40 percent for people with no debt.

Be sure to call previous landlords and references listed. Although not all liars are bad credit risks, bad credit risks often lie.

If you allow pets on your property and it is a condominium, make sure the HOA rules allow this. Some communities only allow small dogs. If your tenant fails to follow the HOA rules, you can be forced to evict them. Be sure they know it's important to follow HOA rules. You can evict them if they fail to follow the rules (this should be part of the lease agreement).

Keep in mind as you review the prospective tenant's credit history that almost everyone is late in paying a bill once in a while. But be wary of those who have filed for bankruptcy, unless it stems from factors out of their control, like medical expenses.

You should also confirm the prospective tenant's employment. If everything looks good, you also might want to interview the tenant. But the Fair Housing Act stipulates that landlords cannot discriminate based upon color, disability, family status, national origin, race, religion, or sex. In addition, much of the information you gather on the background form and background check is private under law. You need to keep it confidential, otherwise you can be sued for invasion of privacy.

4. Use a Legally Valid Lease

A lease agreement requires you to provide a safe and clean home for the tenant, and the tenant must treat the property with respect and pay you for living there.

Although state and federal laws pertaining to lease agreements can be very complicated, many state governments and real estate organizations post sample lease agreements that comply with both state and federal law. These are usually free. You can also pay a private online company to create one tailored to your needs.

To find an agreement online, search "lease agreement for [insert your state]". If you can't find a free one, a $50 fee to buy one from a private company now could save you thousands of dollars in judgments later for violating a law or ordinance.

Here are some of the major items you'll find in a lease agreement:

1. *Property location.*
2. *Rent amount and fees* for late payments.
3. *Term* (length) of lease.
4. *Security Deposit amount*, kinds of deductions that can be applied, such as late rent charges, and how they will be refunded.
5. *Who can use the premises.*
6. *No alterations and improvements* without permission of landlord.
7. *Non-delivery of possession.* Landlord is not liable if the premises become unfit for living for reasons out of the landlord's control.
8. *Condition of premises* at time of leasing.
9. *Non subletting clause.*
10. *Hazardous materials.* Tenant is not allowed to store hazardous materials on the property.
11. *Utilities.* Who is responsible for paying for various utilities? Landlords usually cover sewer, water, and trash pick-up. Tenants usually pay for electricity and natural gas.

12. *Maintenance, repair, and rules.* Tenants are required to keep the property clean and safe and landlord is responsible for repairs not caused by tenant.

13. *Damage to premises.* This item spells out what happens if the property is destroyed by fire or a storm and is uninhabitable.

14. *Access by landlord.* Landlords are required to notify tenants in advance when the former needs access to the rental unit for repairs. But under emergency conditions, landlords in all states can obtain access without tenant approval.

15. *Animals.* Specifies whether animals are allowed and conditions for that arrangement.

16. *Waterbeds.* Waterbeds are prohibited unless landlord approves.

17. *Subordination of lease.* If an entity such as a bank or government agency obtains control over the property and the landlord has no power, the tenant's rights can be terminated.

18. *Quiet enjoyment.* Tenant must respect the privacy of other residents living nearby.

19. *Indemnification.* Tenant agrees to reimburse the landlord for legal and other costs associated with violations of the lease.

After your tenant signs the lease and obtains the keys, ask the tenant to inspect the unit and provide a list of items that need to be repaired. You will make the fixes and then the tenant will sign off on the form. When the lease ends, you have a right to deduct from the security deposit the cost of repairing any damaged items.

5. Treat Tenants with Respect but be Unwavering

If you are a one-tenant landlord, you likely will have an interpersonal relationship with your tenant, and it's great to have a good relationship.

But you and your tenant need to understand each other's roles. Your job is to provide a safe and clean unit and their role is to respect the rules and pay their rent. If your tenant fails to pay on time, you must impose a late fee (deduct this from the security deposit). If you don't, they will assume they can do that again. The maximum fee you can charge is generally no more than 5 percent of the rent (see your state law).

Keep your relationship with your tenants professional. Limit socializing with them (unless they're a relative or close friend, of course). Close friends cut each other slack. But landlords cannot afford to do that. From time to time, you may have to send your tenants legal notices. Don't write your own — use online sources, which provide samples of different types of notices composed by attorneys.

How to Evict a Tenant

Evicting a tenant for nonpayment of rent or violating a rule is expensive, time-consuming, and unpleasant. But a tenant who refuses to leave will wipe out your cash flow.

There are at least five justifiable reasons to evict a tenant.

1. *Nonpayment of Rent.* This the most common reason for evicting tenants, but you can't evict a renter who piles up lots of late fees. As long as they pay they can stay.

2. *Violation of Lease.* A common lease violation is an unauthorized occupant or pet. Lovers often move in without seeking permission from the landlord, but they can pose liability problems for you. Unapproved subletting of the unit also increases liability problems. Rental units are also to be used for residential living only, not for a business.

   A tenant who has a lot of loud parties is also problem and can be evicted, but you need to provide a written warning so you have a record of warnings when you need to evict.

3. *Crime or Drug-Related Activity.* You can easily evict a resident who is selling or using drugs. Some states allow you to terminate a lease with 24-hour notice for crime-related activities.

4. *Damage to Property.* If a tenant does serious damage to your unit and refuses to pay for the damages, you can evict them.

5. *Expiration of Lease.* When the lease expires, the tenant is required to move out, but if they don't and stop paying rent, you can evict them because the tenant no longer has a right to occupy the dwelling.

Eviction rules vary across states. Be sure to follow them closely. Generally, the process involves five steps:

1. Notify the tenant in writing that you're terminating the lease and cite the reason. If they refuse to leave:
2. File an eviction complaint with the local court;
3. Present your evidence at a court hearing;
4. When the court issues the eviction notice, hire a sheriff's deputy, who shows up on eviction day and ensures the tenant leaves;
5. Change the locks on the doors.

The court will issue an eviction notice if the tenant (defendant) fails to appear. Don't turn off utilities or change the locks without a court action. It's illegal. And don't accept payment from your tenant if you have already filed for eviction, because this will nullify the eviction process.

How to Manage a Short-Term Rental

Before I put my Phoenix rental home up for rent, I used online calculators to estimate how much my property would gross as a short-term rental.

The estimates varied wildly, from $20,000 a year gross to $57,000. One produced a fairly accurate estimate of my actual yearly gross ($45,000), but it underestimated my occupancy (67% versus the actual 86%). If I only had only 67 percent occupancy in 2023, my total gross would have been about a third less, or $35,000.[132] That wouldn't have been enough for me to justify renting short term. A long-term rental would produce $30,000 ($2,500 a month), and the $5,000 difference wouldn't have been worth all of the extra work, at least to me.

The lesson here is don't be suckered by these websites. Their primary concern isn't you — it's making money from you. Most of them are fronts for real estate agents and investment companies who are trying to get your business. The only sure way to know whether you can make money leasing short term is through trial and error.

Short-term rentals can be successful in any community or place. But

---

[132]My nightly rates average $137 year-round and are a very good value for the money when compared with upscale hotels and resorts in the Phoenix area, which often charge $300 to $400 or more a night. Upscale hotels offer many perks, but lack a private backyard and swimming pool (surrounded by 6-foot-high cinder block walls).

they tend to do better in areas that draw tourists and visitors.

A good example is Mission Beach in San Diego. The area is jam-packed with short-term condo and home rentals. Tourists go there for the sandy beach, the big waves, and moderately warm temperatures year-round. The area also is packed with restaurants and stores that cater to the short-term visitor. Phoenix is another good place for short-term rentals, because it is warm in the winter and attracts tourists ("snow birds") from the cold northern states.

So if your property is located in an area frequented by tourists, that's a good sign that a short-term rental could do well. In contrast, if your property is located in a small town or rural area that doesn't attract tourists, a long-term lease may be a better option.

But before you purchase a property or turn it into a short-term rental, let's go over some of the benefits and disadvantages of short- versus long-term rentals. Then I'll give you some tips on how to maximize your property's potential as a short-term rental. Finally, I'll show you how to sign up with either Airbnb or Vrbo and make decisions about rental rates, guest rules, and booking policies.

Advantages of Short- versus Long-Term Rentals

There are advantages and disadvantages to leasing either short- or long-term. Table 18.1 summarizes them, and here is an extended discussion of each.

Advantages of Short-Term Rentals

1. *Higher Profit Margins.* As already mentioned, the single biggest advantage that short-term rentals have over long-term is higher profit margins. Many online sites claim you can earn three to five times as

Table 18.1 Advantages of Short- versus Long-Term Rentals		
Short-Term Rental Has Advantage	**Short-Term Rental**	**Long-Term Rental**
1. Higher Profit Margins	**Higher**	Lower
2. Getting Paid on Time	**Higher**	Lower
3. Flexible Pricing	**Yes**	Limited
4. Less Risk of Property Damage	**Lower Risk**	Higher Risk
5. Personal Vacation Use	**Yes**	No
6. Easier to Keep Up with Repairs	**Easier**	More Difficult
7. No Background Check Necessary	**Yes**	No
Long-Term Rental Has Advantage		
1. Consistent Income	Varies	**Higher**
2. Less Work (cleaning, maintenance)	More Work	**Less Work**
3. Lower Operating Costs	Higher Costs	**Lower Costs**
4. Unit Doesn't Need to be Furnished	Does	**Does not**
5. Easier to Get Reimbursed for Damages	Harder	**Easier**
6. Fewer Restrictive Laws/Ordinances	More Restrictions	**Fewer**
7. Fewer Neighbor Complaints	More Complaints	**Fewer**

much as a long-term rental. The best estimate, in my opinion, is two times more. When estimating profit potential, it's better to underestimate than to overestimate. And, as I've said before, if you can't turn a profit on a long-term lease for your property, don't buy it. Short-term rentals can be volatile.

2. *Getting Paid on Time.* This is also a big advantage for short-term rentals. Both Airbnb and Vrbo collect payment from guests in advance and then turn the proceeds over to you, the host, after they arrive. You never have to worry about getting paid. Both companies also pay sales tax and other fees to local and state governments in your area. So you don't have to worry about that.

In contrast, if you have a long-term renter, you have to trust that they will pay you on time every month. Of course, some don't. If they skip two monthly payments, you probably will be in the red financially, because most states limit the size of security deposits that you can charge. They typically are not large enough to cover two missed payments.

Of course, some tenants will pack up and leave without notice. These tenants also tend to leave the place in a mess. The best way to avoid these problems is to carefully screen your tenants and purchase a home in a good market. As noted before, good tenants like good markets.

3. *Flexible Pricing.* A short-term rental gives you more flexibility to change rental rates. If I see that I have some unbooked dates a month or so into the future, I will often drop my rates to entice guests. In contrast, if I see that I'm getting very filled up, I will sometimes increase future rates a bit.

From time to time I also search Airbnb and Vrbo to compare the rates and bookings of my competitors. I often see nice places with few bookings, usually because the landlord is charging too much. When you start out, it's better to go low than high to test the waters. Later you can raise the rates if you are getting a lot of bookings. I started out with $99 a night in June, which is the beginning of the really hot months in Phoenix. My place filled up quickly, so the following summer I increased the rates $20 to $30 a night.

You can also change rental rates on a long-term rental, but you are limited to doing that only when the lease expires or your tenant leaves.

4. *Less Risk of Property Damage.* Because Airbnb and Vrbo guests stay for a shorter period of time, the risk of damage to the property is lower. I have only had three guests in two years who have damaged the property (a screen door, back of the front door, broken lamp, and carpet damage). Two of the guests paid me in cash for the damages. Airbnb reimbursed me for the third guest.[133]

Many long-term rental tenants who damage the property won't tell you about it. They are afraid you will charge them. Of course, you can take it out of the security deposit when they leave, but if the damages are greater than the security deposit, you may have trouble getting fully reimbursed after they leave the property.

5. *Personal Vacation Use.* One advantage of a short-term rental is that you can reserve time for yourself or family and friends on your property. You simply block out the dates on the calendars at Airbnb or Vrbo. By the way, you can lease your property through both services by synchronizing the two calendars. When someone books dates on one calendar, the other will show that the property is not available during that time.

If you have a long-term property, you could book your stay after the tenant leaves, but you may not have control over the time of year the lease expires. If a tenant's lease ends in January in Minnesota, you could book your stay in February — that is, if you love freezing temperatures, snow, and ice. On the other hand, if the property is a cabin on a lake where you could ice fish, that could be a good thing.

6. *Easier to Keep Up with Repairs.* With a short-term rental, you have constant access to your property in-between guests and, thus, can fix things before they turn into big problems. With a long-term rental, you must depend on your tenants to identify problems. Some won't do that, especially if they think they'll be charged for the repairs.

---

[133] Airbnb offers hosts some options for damage reimbursement. I'll talk about that later in this chapter 18.

7. *No Background Check Necessary.* As a short-term landlord, you don't have to worry about background checks if your bookings come from Airbnb or Vrbo. Those firms collect the money through credit card transactions, and they also keep records on guests who violate hosts' policies and guidelines. If a guest has a history of not treating properties with respect, those booking services will block them. The credit card transaction also gives the booking services the ability to track down guests who engage in fraudulent activities or destructive behaviors.

Advantages of Long-Term Rentals

1. *Consistent Income.* A key advantage of a long-term rental is that the income is consistent as long as the tenant keeps paying the rent. You know that you will get a monthly payment and how much it will be. You know precisely how much revenue you will generate in a year.

   In contrast, short-term property owners don't know precisely how much revenue they will produce each month or in a year. Guests sometimes cancel their bookings, which means you can lose revenue unexpectedly at any time. One way to limit the impact of this is to create a moderately strong cancellation policy. I offer a full refund 30 days or more in advance, and 50 percent up to 14 days. No refund after that.

   Airbnb and Vrbo encourage you to offer a full refund within days of the reservation. But that just entices guests who are unsure about coming. These wishy-washy guests often cancel at the last minute. I don't want guests who aren't committed to coming, so I have very few cancellations — maybe one out of 15.

2. *Less Work.* A long-term rental is less work than a short-term one. You don't have to clean the unit every time a guest leaves. Typically, you will clean once a year, after a tenant leaves the property. A short-term rental also tends to have more maintenance, as you will find things that

need fixing more frequently. But sometimes fixing the small problems saves money in the long run, because small problems don't become big ones if they are fixed sooner.

3. *Lower Operating Costs.* With a long-term rental, your tenants typically will pay utility costs, including electricity, gas, internet, and cable TV or streaming service costs. You normally will pay for trash pickup, water, and sewer costs. The cost of utilities can be high. On my property, I pay an average of $400+ for utilities each month. The cost of electricity, which is the main source of heating and cooling in Arizona, is high. These costs drop considerably during the mild winter months, but I offer a free heated swimming pool (heat pump), so that keeps my costs fairly high year-round.

4. *Unit Doesn't Need to be Furnished.* Short-term landlords must furnish the properties they lease with furniture, beds, dishes, televisions, towels, supplies (paper towels, soaps, etc.). It cost me about $6,000 to furnish my Phoenix condo. That's a substantial cost. Long-term landlords don't have to concern themselves with these matters. If a guest brings in bedbugs, then you might have to purchase all new beds and carpeting. So there are more risks in short-term rentals.

5. *Easier to Get Reimbursed for Damages.* A long-term landlord has the benefit of obtaining a security deposit from the tenant. This makes it easier to be reimbursed when a tenant damages something on the property. Airbnb and Vrbo offer various programs to get reimbursed for damages, but some of them force guests to pay a small insurance fee to cover damages. That may hurt your occupancy rate.

6. *Fewer Restrictive Laws/Ordinances.* Many cities and communities in recent years have placed increasingly rigid rules on short-term rentals, including fines for violating noise standards. People who live in residential neighborhoods can be very unwelcoming to homeowners

who lease their properties, especially short-term. Cities also often require owners of short-term rentals to register their property. This enables the cities to makes it easier to police the property and to obtain sales taxes on the bookings.

7. *Fewer Neighbor Complaints.* In the early years of online short-term rental bookings, many guests would lease a property for a night or two and would throw big parties, where the party-goers would often trash the home. These parties also generated a lot of loud noise complaints from neighbors. In response, the booking services changed their policies and now monitor guests more closely. Local governments also began cracking down on short-term rentals, some even banning them altogether. Today, there are fewer problems, but short-term rentals still generate more complaints than long-term rentals. Long-term tenants realize that they can be kicked out of their rental unit if they fail to follow the lease and laws.

Maximizing the Appeal of Your Short-Term Rental

When I decided to lease my Phoenix home as a short-term rental, I was worried about how people would perceive it. My home is modest. It has a large heated swimming pool, but it doesn't have granite countertops or a swanky interior.

My home doesn't look like the properties that Airbnb and Vrbo often promote, which offer a high number of amenities, including gorgeous swimming pools, hot tubs, granite or quartz countertops, beautifully decorated interiors, and gorgeous exteriors. The nightly rates on these homes were high. So I thought my property, which had rates closer to a mid-priced motel, would receive lower ratings than those gorgeous homes.

I was wrong.

Guest after guest kept giving my property 5.0 ratings. I now have nearly 80 total ratings from both Airbnb and Vrbo and only one of them is less than 5.0 (one 4.0 rating). So how do you get high ratings?

Cleanliness, Problem Solving, Communicating

I made sure my home was extremely clean before a guest arrived. A dirty rental is the fastest way to get low ratings.

I also responded to potential and actual guests as quickly as I could. When they booked, I sent a thank you message and gave them my phone number so they could text or call if they had questions. (Most would continue to communicate through the booking services, which was okay.)

If a problem came up (like the swimming pool not heating properly), I was on it immediately. If they needed my assistance, I drove over there right away. (My condo home is only 8 minutes away.)

I enjoyed talking with the guests. That, no doubt, also helped me get higher ratings. Meeting the landlord and discovering that he's just an ordinary guy trying to achieve financial freedom makes him more human, in contrast to corporate hotels that are professionally managed.

Guests would routinely tell me "your house is beautiful." Of course, my point of comparison was the upscale homes in Scottsdale and other areas of Phoenix.

My house is also showing its age. Some internal walls need to be repainted. Guests' dogs have clawed away at the back of the front door trying to get out while their owners were away. (I no longer allow pets.) And the carpeting in the living room and bedrooms soon will need to be replaced.

But guests didn't seem to care.

And many made another comment that I now think is the main factor driving my high ratings.

Homey Is the Key

"Your place is homey," they would say. "Very comfortable. I feel like I'm at home."

The dictionary defines hominess as "a feeling of home; comfortable; cozy." Many short-term rentals, however, are filled with cheap furniture and have few knick-knacks. They're spartan. The warmth is missing.

In contrast, I left almost everything in the home before I leased it: furniture, CDs, books, DVDs, wall pictures and metal artwork, artificial plants, stereos, and rugs. In the living room, I left a new comfortable sofa and a La-Z-Boy rocker. The dining room table was 20 years old but was made of teak, which gives off a warm glow. The family/TV room had an L-shaped sofa and a nice throw rug, in addition to teak bookshelves. The shelves were adorned with pottery and stuff I had collected on my trips to other countries throughout the world.

I installed high quality memory foam toppers on two of the three beds. Guests constantly tell me that the beds are comfortable. You don't even need an expensive mattress. Buy an inexpensive but firm mattress. The memory foam makes every bed feel comfortable. (The mattress in the third bedroom has no memory foam to accommodate those who prefer a firmer surface.)

In addition, furnish your place with everything a guest will need to stay there. This includes paper towels, laundry soap, dish and dishwasher soaps, hand soap, bar soap, toilet paper, shampoos and conditioners, napkins, salt and pepper, and cleaning supplies. I supply these things for all guests, no matter how long they stay. Include an iron and ironing board, a crock pot, and lots of dishes and silverware. They don't have to match. Guests don't care a lot about that. The only thing I don't supply is food or bottled water or drinks, but guests don't expect these items.

I know it costs extra to supply the rental. But it really pays off. I even supply coffee for both the conventional drip coffee machine and the one-cup-at-a-time machine. If guests get in late at night, they don't have to go to the store in the morning to buy coffee. Many people need their coffee in the morning.

Even if you do all of this, I can't guarantee you'll get 5.0 ratings. But stocking your short-term rental property and making your property homey certainly won't generate lower ratings.

How to Sign Up with Airbnb and Vrbo

Registering your property with Airbnb and/or Vrbo is not difficult. But it does take some time to learn how to navigate the two websites.

Before you sign up, here's a few things you will need:

1. *Identification* (usually a driver's license).
2. Your *Employer Identification Number* (EIN) or your *Social Security number*. You don't have to create a limited liability company or partnership. You can register as a sole proprietor.
3. A *bank account* connected to your EIN or Social Security number. You will need this to receive payments from the two booking companies. The deposits normally will be electronically delivered into your checking account.
4. A *credit card*, which is used to cover unexpected expenses and shortfalls in your account. But normally your account is not debited. I have never been billed by either company.
5. A *brief description of your property* that promotes your property as a great place to stay. Also reference the amenities that your property offers.
6. *Twenty to 50 pictures* of your property. You can use your phone and download them directly to your listing, or upload through your desktop. In general, it's easier to navigate the websites through a desktop, because you can see more options.

Setting Up Your Page

Setting up your short-term rental property page involves six steps or thereabouts.

1. *Create an Account.* The first step is to create an account. It will take a couple of days to link the account to your bank account. Meanwhile, you can continue setting up your listing. The software interfaces at both booking companies will walk you through the process.

2. *Describe Your Property.* Give a name to your property and/or create a headline for your listing. I used "Dave's Sunshine Getaway/Free Heated Pool/Full Home." I added the "full home" after I received inquiries about whether the property contained more than one rental unit. Many short-term hosts bill guests for heating the pool. I have a heat pump, as opposed to gas or electric heating, which is much less expensive.

   Airbnb limits the number of characters hosts can use to describe their property. So focus on what's unique and wonderful about your space. Is your property near some popular tourist sites? Or convention centers? Or shopping areas and restaurants? Vrbo gives you more space to describe your property, so you can provide more information, such as listing some of the special sights to see in the area or additional amenities in your house. Here's what I wrote for Airbnb:

   > Great value for the money. This 3-bedroom, 1,920-sq-ft home with a 15-by-35 heated swimming pool (great for water volleyball and laps) is located in north central Phoenix, putting it within 30 minutes or less from Scottsdale, downtown Phoenix, Tempe, Sun City, Chandler. Middle-class neighborhood with a park one block south. Lots of shopping, restaurants. Full kitchen, free Amazon TV and Netflix. Free Wifi and Foosball table. Washer/dryer. 3-day min. stay; $125 cleaning fee.

3. *Upload Photographs.* The software interface will then ask you to upload photographs. Include pictures of the outside of the property and in each room, showing everything from different angles. You can also create a virtual tour. Your first picture on your page is the most important, because that's the one potential guests will see first. I used my swimming pool, which is much bigger than a typical pool. It is rectangular and has a volleyball net across the middle. Almost every guest who comes to my property does so in part because of the pool.

4. *Provide Details about Rooms and House.* The software systems also will ask you to provide details about each room, including sleeping arrangements, size of beds, number of bathrooms, whether you accept pets, your cleaning fee, other fees that you would like to charge.

5. *Create House Rules.* You can also create your own house rules, such as no smoking, no loud noises in the backyard after 10 p.m. Text Box 18.1 on the next page presents a summary of my guidebook, which lists some of the rules and instructions for operating devices in my rental.

6. *Set Your Nightly Rate.* The booking services typically will suggest a nightly rate based on factors like location, amenities, and guest demand. These suggested rates are not always suitable, but you can change the price anytime later. The only exception is when a guest books the room. That rate is a binding contract and you can't change it.

One approach to set your rate is to determine how much the nightly rate would be if you rented the property long term, then double it. You can also look at the rates charged by other properties near yours. To do this, you can pretend to be a customer on the sites and identify the city or community in which you would like to book. Be sure to compare only homes or condos that have the same number of rooms and bathrooms as your place. Airbnb also has a Smart Pricing tool, which automatically adjusts your nightly price based on demand. I don't use it because I want to acquire the knowledge to set my own prices. I often

---

Text Box 18.1
Dave's Sunshine Getaway Guidebook

David Demers, owner (Phone number; Email address)

(Short Introduction) I purchased the home you are staying in ten years ago, when my daughter and I moved here. I took early retirement. I worked as a professor, newspaper reporter, and book publisher (still have the company). ... As you can see, the home is not a designer home, but it's very comfortable, in our opinion. I hope you enjoy it as much as we have.

DO NOT WASH THE SHEETS OR TOWELS BEFORE YOU LEAVE. THAT'S OUR JOB. BUT PLEASE CLEAN THE GAS GRILL IF YOU USE IT.

Wifi Password
Front Door Entry Code (normally the last digits of your telephone number you listed at Airbnb or Vrbo). This entry code is changed after every guest visit. To open the front door, enter the four-digit code above and press the oval key above the numbered keys. To lock the door, hold down any numbered key for 2 seconds.

(Summary of subheads, each of which have an extended discussion)
Emergency Number: 911
Swimming Pool: Rules and No Diving Warning (pool is 3.5 to 4.5 feet deep)
Water Shutoff Valve: Where to find it if a pipe breaks
Refrigerator: How to operate the ice maker
AC/Heat: How the air conditioning and heating systems work
Foosball Room: How to enjoy the game
Television: How to operate the TV (which has Amazon Prime and Netflix)
Supplies: Types of supplies provided
Garbage: Where to deposit the garbage and how to recycle
Laundry: How to operate the washer and dryer
Dishwasher: How to operate
Security: Outdoor lighting and door locks to protect the property
Books, CDs, and Games: Where they are stored
Bugs: How to deal with bugs (e.g., don't leave the sliding glass door open)
Charges for Damages to Things: My policy on damages
Checking Out Instructions: How to check out

I hope you enjoy your stay. If you have any questions, please contact me. -Dave

change them when I have too few or too many bookings (decreasing the price in the former and raising it in the latter).

You should consider offering discounts and promotions to attract your first guests. Both services allow you to deduct 20 percent off your nightly price for your first three bookings. You can also set up discounts for weekly and monthly stays. I offer a 10 percent discount for 7 days or more and 15 percent for 28 days or more.

How and When You're Paid

The booking services collect payment from the guests (usually through a credit card) before they arrive. They send your share of the booking a day or so after the guest's scheduled check-in time. You get payment for your full nightly rate plus any additional fees you charge (such as a cleaning fee), minus any discounts you give.

If there are any local or state taxes for short-term stays, the booking services collect those fees and pay them directly to the governing agency. That can vary depending on jurisdiction. For bookings of a month (28 to 30 days, depending on state laws) or more, sales taxes are not normally collected. This is considered a long-term stay in most jurisdictions. (Note: Renters throughout the country normally do not have to pay sales taxes.)

The booking services charge you a small fee for processing the payment or a host service fee (1.5% to 3%). The guest also is billed an additional service fee that goes to the booking service (10% to 12%). All told, the booking services typically add about 12 to 15 percent to the total nightly bill.

The booking services offer different payout methods, including direct deposit to a checking account, PayPal, and Western Union. Direct deposit is the most popular. You can change your payment method any time.

Getting Ready for Your Guests

Most hosts now use an electronic deadbolt lock on the front or entry door, which means the guest just punches in four numbers or so and the door opens. It's very convenient for you and the guest. No lost keys to deal with. Most hosts set the code to the last four digits of the telephone number of the guest, which is available after they book.

By the way, keep the batteries in the electronic lock fresh. I had one that corroded and the lock stopped working. The guests couldn't get in and called me, but I had turned my phone off that night. They spent the night in a hotel, and I was obligated to pay their hotel fees.

Here are some other tips for welcoming and helping your guests:

1. Be sure to text them in advance through the booking services, giving them step-by-step information about how and where to enter your home. I usually do this about a week in advance. Guests tend to get a little antsy before their scheduled trip. Waiting to give them check-in information the night before is too late unless you give advance notice.

2. Be sure they have your phone number so they can contact you directly. Most will still communicate through the booking services' texting systems, which will automatically notify you through your phone. But in an emergency, a direct call is often the fastest way for them to notify you. They also feel more comfortable knowing you have a number through which they can reach you directly.

   You need to be available 24/7 in case an emergency arises. That means you need to leave your phone on during the middle of the night. As I noted above, I failed to do that and it cost me about $250 to rent rooms for my guests who were locked out of the house.

3. Respond as quickly as you can to their concerns. Failure to respond in a swift manner can earn you low reviews.

4. Most guests don't care whether you are on the premises when they arrive. Some prefer you not there. Others will love to meet you. Be pleasant and helpful, of course. I have always had wonderful conversations with guests. These conversations also make them feel comfortable, and no doubt they contribute to higher reviews.

5. Create and provide a brief guidebook in the house so they know your house rules and how to run equipment, such as the swimming pool waterfall. A summary of my guidebook and its section headings are available in Text Box 18.1.

Short-Term Rental Insurance

Airbnb and Vrbo provide hosts with $1 million in liability coverage. But you still need to purchase landlord insurance to cover the house or condo itself, and it's a good idea to purchase another $300,000 in liability coverage. When you buy the insurance, be sure to tell the company that you are leasing your property short-term. The rates are slightly higher than long-term rental coverage, but you want to be sure you get reimbursed should a liability claim emerge.

Airbnb also provides $3 million in host damage protection. You're reimbursed if your guest causes damage to your home and belongings, including parked cars and boats, and the insurance also covers you if you need to cancel another confirmed booking because of damages caused by a guest or invitees. Acts of nature are excluded.

How to Do Your Books

Y ou've converted your home into a rental or purchased a new property and your first renter or guest is staying at the place and you've already got a pile of receipts for expenses.

You know what you need to do next.

But you're not happy about it.

You're not alone.

Few people enjoy bookkeeping.

Many even find it intimidating.

But keeping track of your financial records isn't difficult. All you need to do is sort your receipts into two piles: one for income (revenue) and one for expenditures (costs). To obtain a general idea of your cash flow or profit, or to file your taxes at the end of the year, you simply deduct the expenses from your income.

You don't have to hire expensive accountants or purchase an expensive and complicated bookkeeping software program, many of which require you to pay a monthly fee of $15 to $250 and may take years to master.[134]

You don't have to use a formal bookkeeping system, especially if

---

[134]QuickBooks is the most widely used accounting system in the United States. As of this writing, an online version of QuickBooks was available for $15 to $100 a month, and if you want assistance you have to pay another $50 a month.

you just have one or two properties.[135] But you do have to manage your finances in order to file your taxes, obtain loans for additional property purchases, and sell your property.

In this chapter, I'll introduce some simple accounting methods and terms as well as offer some tips on how to reduce your tax bill.

Bookkeeping in Three Steps

Bookkeeping can be broken down into three basic steps:

1. Select an Accounting Method

You must choose either *cash* or *accrual*. This is not an option. The IRS requires you to use one method or the other. Cash is the simpler for small real estate businesses. You record income when you deposit it and expenses when pay them. Then, at tax time, you fill out the tax forms using an electronic software program (see next section for details). The software will ask you to list your sources of income and expenses.

The accrual method is more complicated. You record income and expenses when you incur them, regardless of when you receive the money or pay the bill. With this method, a company can show a profit even though revenues may be less than expenses. The accrual method is used by bigger businesses.

2. Select an Accounting System

If your business is growing or becoming more complex, you will need to use an accounting software system or hire a bookkeeper and/or

---

[135]I create a table in WordPerfect and use simple formula commands to sum, subtract and multiply. Any spreadsheet program will also work.

Certified Public Account to keep track of your records. This is necessary so you can file your taxes and obtain loans and other services from lending institutions.

The language of accounting can be complicated, but you don't need to learn everything to be a competent real estate entrepreneur. I've narrowed it down to 21 key terms, many of which are already familiar to you (see Text Box 19.1).

3. Record Income and Expenses

After selecting your method and system of accounting, record your income and expenses.

- *Income.* With respect to rental properties, the IRS defines income as normal rent payments, advance rent payments, payments for canceling a lease, and expenses paid by the tenant. Rental income does not include a security deposit if the taxpayer intends to return it to the tenant at the end of the lease. But if the taxpayer keeps part or all of the deposit, because the tenant failed to follow the terms of the lease, then the retained amount is income.

- *Tax Deductible Expenses.* Expenses are either deductible or depreciable. Tax deductible expenses include interest payments on a mortgage, phone and utilities (portion used for business), transportation, business/office meals (50 percent deductible), company-wide party (100 percent deductible), supplies and materials for repairs and maintenance, and use of vehicle. Always keep receipts.

- *Depreciable Expenses.* These include start-up expenses for your business (before you begin renting your property), remodeling projects, and loan closing costs (which are part of the capital costs of a property). Start-up costs are depreciated over 15 years, but new businesses can

Text Box 19.1
Common Accounting Terms

Accounts Payable: Bills that haven't been paid.

Accounts Receivable: Sales or income (such as rent) not yet been collected.

Accrued Expense: A bill that hasn't been paid.

Asset: Anything that has monetary value, from cash to land.

Balance Sheet: A financial statement that lists assets, liabilities, and equity. Also called an *equity statement.*

Cash Flow: The inflow and outflow of cash in a business. A positive number indicates that more cash flowed in than out of the business. This implies a profit, but a negative cash flow doesn't necessarily mean the business is not making money. Appreciation can offset a negative cash flow.

Depreciation: The loss of value in an asset over time. An asset generally has to have substantial value to warrant depreciating it.

Equity: The value of a business or property after liabilities have been subtracted from assets *(Equity = Assets - Liabilities).*

Expense: A cost incurred.

Fixed Cost: A cost that doesn't change as a result of other conditions. The opposite of a fixed cost is a variable cost.

Income Statement: A financial statement showing revenues, expenses, and profits over a given time period. Also called a *profit and loss statement.*

Invoice: A bill that seeks payment from a person who owes money.

Liability: Debts to be paid. Common liabilities include accounts payable and loans *(Liabilities = Assets - Equity).*

Liquidity: The speed at which something of value can be converted into cash.

Net Income: The dollar amount earned in profits. Net income is calculated by taking revenue and subtracting all of the expenses in a given period (such as a month or year).

Net Margin: The percent amount reflecting the profit of a company in relation to its revenue. It's calculated by dividing net income and by revenue for a given period.

Overhead: Expenses involved in running a business that do not include the making or delivering of the product or service. Rent and salaries are included in overhead.

Profit: The financial benefit realized when revenue gained from a business activity exceeds expenses and taxes.

Profit and Loss Statement: See "Income Statement."

Revenue: Sales or income earned in a given time period.

Variable Cost: Costs that change with the volume of sales (opposite of *fixed cost*).

deduct $5,000. Anything over that must be depreciated. So, if you spend $7,500 before you listed your property for rent, you can deduct $5,000 from your rental income immediately and the other $2,500 will be depreciated over 15 years, which means you only get to deduct $167 each year ($2,500 ÷ 1/15).

Remodeling expenses exclude repairs to the property, such as fixing a leaking sink. Those can be fully deducted. But when you remodel a kitchen or bathroom, you have to depreciate those costs over 27.5 years, because they are a capital improvement. They add value to your property. So if the remodeling project costs $27,500, you can only deduct $1,000 a year from your income.

In terms of loan closing costs, you can only deduct home mortgage interest and annual real estate taxes. Other costs — such as legal fees, abstract/recording fees, title search and document preparation, land surveys, title insurance, transfer or stamp taxes, expenses you paid for the seller, points you paid to reduce the interest rate on your mortgage loan, easement payments — must be depreciated, usually over 27.5 years.[136]

- *Deducting Vehicle Expenses.* Vehicle expenses associated with your business can be deducted. You have two options: *standard-mileage* and *actual expenses.*

  In 2023, the standard-mileage option allows you to deduct 65.5 cents for every mile you drive for business. The alternative method for "writing off your vehicle" is the actual expense method, which involves deducting actual costs for maintaining a vehicle. This would include gas and oil, tires, repairs, fees and taxes, insurance, loan interest, depreciation, and parking fees.

  In general, the more economical your vehicle is to operate, the more likely the standard mileage rate will give you a bigger deduction. But the expense method requires you to drive at least half of the miles for

---

[136]I highly recommend Stephen Fishman's *Every Landlord's Tax Deduction Guide* (Berkeley, CA: Nolo).

business. If you don't drive that much, you'll have to use the standard-mileage method. If you choose to use the standard-mileage method in the first year, you can switch to actual expenses later. But once you start or switch to actual expenses, you can't choose standard-mileage later.

In either case, you'll need to keep track of the miles you drive for business. There are a number of apps that will record your mileage, or you can simply record it on paper. You'll record the day, time, odometer reading start and finish, and purpose of trip. To use the actual expense method, keep all of your receipts. At the end of the year, you calculate the proportion of miles spent driving for business and that's the percentage you get to deduct from all auto expenses.

If you're unsure which method gives you the best result, tax software programs can select the one most beneficial to you.

Double-Entry Bookkeeping

The simple way to do the books is to create two piles of receipts: one for your income and another for expenses. This is called *single-entry method of accounting.*

Most small-time real estate landlords use this method. But if you own more properties, keeping track of the profitability of your business can be more difficult, especially when you sell a property in a year other than when it was purchased, or when expenses and income are recorded in the year before or after the sale.

The *double-entry method of accounting* solves this problem. Every time an income or expense occurs, the *balance sheet* (also called equity statement or net worth statement) is updated right away. Under the single entry method, the balance sheet is usually updated only once a year, at tax time.

In double entry, the balance sheet is created based on actual costs, not market values. So your net worth changes as a result of profit or loss. If you are confused (like me), don't worry. Accounting can be complex.

Of course, I can't teach you how to use double-entry accounting (hiring an accountant is the best way to do that). The double-entry method is preferred by investors or financial institutions when you seek a loan. They want to see how profitable your business is today, not wait until the end of the year.

How to File Your Taxes

Nothing is certain but death and taxes.

Ben Franklin and several other writers popularized that phrase.

Today I suspect some real estate investors would, figuratively speaking, prefer death to taxes, at least when they are doing them on the night before the deadline.

Filing taxes can be nerve-wracking.[137]

But if you kept all of your receipts, doing your taxes isn't difficult. And you don't have to hire an expensive accountant or tax attorney.

If you make less than $73,000, you can use free online software (https://apps.irs.gov/app/freeFile).[138] Alternatively, you can purchase for under $100 a tax software program, such as TurboTax (you'll need the "Home and Business" version). I've used it for more than 15 years.

These programs take you through the filing process step by step. All you have to do is answer the questions. Normally, it is easy. But I'll be honest and tell you that you probably will run into a couple of situations

---

[137]Maurie Backman, "Most Americans Think Filing Taxes Is Stressful — But It Doesn't Have to Be," *The Motley Fool* (January 30, 2018), retrieved October 27, 2020, from <https://www.fool.com/retirement/ 2018/01/30/most-americans-think-filing-taxes-is-stressful-but.aspx>.

[138]Note that these free tax programs are offered by private companies who may try to charge you for filing for state income tax return and sell you other services. High-income tax filers may not be eligible for the free software.

where you are not sure what to do. I research online and usually can find the solutions. But the more you use these software programs, the easier they are to do. And it can save you hundreds of dollars in accounting fees and make you a smarter business person.

Schedule E

If you own and rent a property, the IRS requires you to file a Schedule E Form (Supplemental Income and Loss) along with your Form 1040 at the end of the year.[139] In online tax programs, you'll find Schedule E under "Business Income and Expenses."

Are You A Real Estate Professional?

One of the first things the tax program asks is whether you're a real estate professional. If you are, you get a tax advantage when your costs exceed your revenues. You get to write off the losses from your other (earned) income. But to quality as a professional, you must meet all three of these requirements:

1. More than half of the personal services you provided during the year were performed in a real property trade or business in which you *materially participated.* This means you actually worked on the property and were not just a *passive* recipient of income from it.

2. The number of hours in which you materially participated in this real property trade or business has to exceed 750 and you must have records of this work.

---

[139]You can find a PDF of Schedule E at this IRS website: <https://www.irs.gov/pub/irs-pdf/f1040se.pdf>.

3. If you have more than one property, you must show that you materially (actively) participated in each rental real estate activity, or you can group all rental real estate activities as one and participate in that grouped activity.

In other words, if your full-time job is renting and maintaining rental properties, you qualify as a real estate professional. If you have another job and just purchased your first rental property, you do NOT qualify as a professional. But don't freak out about this. The tax law will still be kind to you if earn less than $150,000 a year.

If you have a part-time job but spend most of your time on your real estate property, then it comes down to how much time you spent working that job versus your rentals and whether you can meet the 750-hour requirement. That's about 15 hours per week.

The upshot is that real estate professionals get a tax advantage over *higher-income* nonprofessional investors. If professionals report losses in their rentals (very common because of depreciation and maintenance and mortgage interest costs), they can deduct those losses from income they receive from other sources.

But nonprofessionals can't take such deductions if their yearly income exceeds $150,000 (modified adjusted gross income[140]). The maximum allowable deduction is the total rental income they receive. So, if their rental earns $10,000 and their expenses are $15,000, they cannot deduct the $5,000 difference this year. But they can carry that loss over to another year and deduct it when their income from the rental exceeds their expenses.

---

[140]Modified adjusted gross income is the money you earn through wages, interest, dividends, rental and royalty income, capital gains, business income, farm income, unemployment, alimony, Social Security, tax-exempt interest, and foreign income and housing costs for qualified individuals — minus contributions to Individual Retirement Accounts, moving expenses, alimony paid, self-employment taxes, and student loan interest.

If, in the years that follow, their rental income never exceeds expenditures, then the carryovers will accumulate until the property is sold. Then they can be deducted, reducing their capital gains taxes.[141]

The problem of expenses being greater than income is usually greatest in the year the property is purchased, because the buyer typically spends a lot on repairs and maintenance and also can depreciate or deduct closing costs and expenses. The conventional wisdom is that investors want to take as many deductions as they can now rather than later, because *a dollar today is worth more than a dollar tomorrow* (inflation makes dollars in the future less valuable).

If you earn less than $150,000 a year, the law gives you a break, because it wants to encourage lower-income people to invest in real estate and climb the economic ladder. If you earn less than $100,000, you get to deduct up to $25,000 in rental property losses from any other income you earn. If your losses exceed $25,000, you can carry them over future years or until you sell your property. If your income is between $100,000 and $150,000, the amount you can deduct is prorated. It declines to zero as your income climbs to $150,000. But, again, you get to carry over those losses to future years.

The upshot is that the tax law is very favorable toward real estate investors, including small-time operators like me.

Your Property Profile

After asking about your professional status, the tax program will ask you for information about your rental property (address, when you purchased it, and whether the income you earned from it came from a

---

[141]When you buy properties, keep each as a separate business. If you pool your properties together under one LLC, you won't be able to take the carryover loss until you sell all of the properties.

1099 tax form). Unless you're a *passive investor* in a real estate venture, you won't receive a 1099 form, because your income comes directly from your tenants or renters.

Income and Expenditures

After submitting profile information, the software asks you to provide your rental income. This includes rent payments from tenants or guests, security deposits you have on file (when you give the deposits back they are recorded as an expense), repairs made by tenants in lieu of rent, and personal goods and services exchanged for rent.

In terms of costs and expenditures, the program will ask you to provide the amounts you spent on advertising to find a tenant, on travel (but don't include auto mileage, which is calculated separately), cleaning/ maintenance (yard grooming, pest control, pool cleaning), insurance, professional fees, management fees, repairs, supplies, taxes, and utilities (gas, electric, water, sewer, garbage collection).

If you have a mortgage on the property, you'll input the lender's name and the amount of interest paid. You'll get this information from a 1098 tax form that the lender will send you at the beginning of a new tax year.

If you purchased the property during the year, the program also will ask you to provide amounts for the abstract, legal and recording fees; title search and document preparation; land survey; title insurance; transfer or stamp taxes; expenses you paid for the seller; points you paid to reduce the interest rate on your mortgage loan; easement payments, energy credits, and energy subsidies.

Some of these closing costs must be depreciated. The program will automatically do that for you. And you also can list other expenses not included in those already mentioned.

Calculating Depreciation

The software program automatically calculates depreciation for your rental property. This includes the cost of the buildings and improvements as well as closing costs associated with the purchase of the property. The program will ask you for the price you paid for the property and the value of the land (land cannot be depreciated, so it is deducted from the selling price of the property before calculating the depreciation).

Some states or jurisdictions, like Arizona, don't require separate values for the land and buildings on residential property. If the appraisal doesn't provide a breakout, you can generally assign 20 percent to the land and 80 percent to the improvements. But if the land area is very small relative to the buildings, then hire an appraiser to determine the split, which could reduce your taxes even more.

The software also will ask you to list the amount you spent on remodeling, room additions, and special tax assessments (such as sewer line hookups). As noted earlier, these expenditures must be depreciated over 27.5 years, because they are capital improvements. Repairs are deducted because they just bring the property back to its useable condition. They don't add value to the property.

Other big ticket purchase items — like refrigerators, stoves, washers, dryers — also may be depreciated over time (the schedule varies by item; see Table 20.1 for a list of some of the items). However, items in the first two rows, which are not affixed to the land, also may be deducted under 2018 IRS rules (Section 179).

Tax law allows small businesses to deduct up to $1.16 million. The decision on whether to use 179 depends on whether the immediate deduction would be financially beneficial to you, compared with spreading it out over a number of years.

The tax program will then calculate the total depreciation.

Table 20.1
IRS Rental Property Depreciation Guidelines

1. Appliances, carpeting and furniture	5 Years
2. Office furniture & equipment	7 Years
3. Fences and roads	15 Years
4. Residential rental buildings, structures, furnaces, water pipes	27.5 Years
5. Commercial buildings	39 Years

Note: The first two items in the table also can be fully deducted under Section 179. The others must be deducted over the time periods shown. For a complete list of items eligible for depreciation, see <https://uphelp.org/wp-content/uploads/2020/09/Depreciation_CP-2.pdf>.

If you purchased after January 1, the program will prorate the depreciation. If you purchased on July 1, which is halfway through the year, you'll get 50 percent of the depreciation. Next year you'll get the full 100 percent.

Preparing 1099 Forms

When you hire workers to perform services that cost $600 or more during the year for your business and they are not a corporation (either C or S), you are required by law to send them a 1099 form (usually a Non Employee Compensation [NEC] form). You also will notify the IRS that you paid them, which helps ensure they pay taxes on the income.

These workers are *independent contractors*, because they control their work (use their own tools and supplies) and don't depend on you for benefits like a pension plan and insurance, as do employees. The 1099 form is sent to independent contractors who operate as sole proprietorships, partnerships, and limited liability companies.

If you pay an independent contractor less than $600 a year, you don't have to report that expense on a 1099 form. The contractor is responsible for reporting the income to the IRS. The 1099 form is available in home and business tax software programs and is easy to complete.

When you hire independent contractors, you'll ask them to complete a W-9 form, which is available at <https://www.irs.gov/pub/irs-pdf/fw9.pdf>. You shouldn't pay them until you get the form, which provides you with their Employer Identification Number or a Social Security number and their address. Of course, you are required under law to keep their Social Security number confidential.

The 1099 forms must be mailed to your contractors before February 1. At the same time, you'll send the IRS a 1099 report that includes a list of all the contractors and the amounts you paid them. If you have employees, you also must withhold federal and state income tax, Social Security, and Medicare from their wages and send these withholdings to the IRS. You probably will need the assistance of an accountant to do this.

The Home Office Deduction

If you use a home office to do your books and other work associated with your rental business, you can deduct that as an expense. Again, the tax software programs will guide you.

The office can be a freestanding structure on your property, such as a studio or garage, or you can use one of the rooms in your apartment or house. You must use that space exclusively for business or for storing tools, inventory, or materials related to your business. A bedroom cannot be used as an office unless you divide the space.[142]

---

[142]An exception is made for some business activities, such as caring for elderly or handicapped people in your home.

One way to calculate the office deduction is take the square footage of the space and multiply it by the IRS-prescribed rate, which currently is $5 a square foot for up to 300 square feet. A more difficult approach involves adding up your overall residential expenses (electricity, natural gas, water and sewer usage, mortgage interest, maintenance, internet, insurance, and repairs) to deduct them from your taxes based on an amount equivalent to the percentage of space your office occupies relative to your entire home or apartment. In other words, if your residential expenses for the entire year are $5,000 and your office takes up 10 percent of the space in your home, your deduction is $500. A third method is to take a straight $500 deduction for the office, which is easy to do but may give you the lowest deduction.

Although the actual expenses method often produces more savings for you, please note that you might have to pay a capital gains tax when you sell your home. You are required to depreciate the value of your home, which means that if you use 5 percent of it for an office, 5 percent of your profit on the home's sale is now subject to capital gains tax.

Meals and Entertainment

The IRS used to be very generous when it came to paying for meals and entertainment expenses. Some meals still qualify. But entertainment expenses no longer do. It has removed many deductions and knocked the business meal deduction down to 50 percent. Table 20.2 shows the deductions. To qualify for a deduction:

- The meal expense must be ordinary and necessary in carrying on your trade or business.
- You, as the business owner, or your employee must be present during the business meal with at least one other party present, such as a client or colleague. This rule is not necessary when you or your employees are

Table 20.2

IRS Rules on Meal Deductions

Entertainment expenses (concerts, golfing, sporting events, etc.)	0%
Meals, groceries, and snacks, for family or self	0%
Business meals with clients	50%
Meals with employees and/or contractors (employees other than yourself and if less than 50% of staff are present)	50%
Meals while traveling for business or conferences	50%
Office snacks (does not apply to S-corp owner if the only employee)	50%
Entertainment-related meals (must be charged separately from other entertainment costs)	50%
Meals with employees and/or contractors (employees other than yourself and if more than 50% of staff are present)	100%
Food for company holiday parties	100%
Food and beverages given free to the public	100%

traveling for business or conferences.
- The meal expense cannot be lavish or extravagant.
- You must keep a proper record of the business meal, including (a) the amount of expense (delivery fees, tips, and sales tax can be included), (b) the time and place of the expense, (c) the business purpose of the expense, and (d) the business relationship to the taxpayer of the individuals being entertained.

Of course, taking large deductions for meals may trigger an IRS audit, which can be a very arduous and time-consuming process.

Part VII

How to Grow Your Rental Business

How to Buy Your Next Rental

As I noted in the first chapter, I am not interested in becoming a wealthy real estate entrepreneur. But if you want to grow your real estate rental business and become a mogul, more power to you.

Just one cautionary note.

The real wealth in our lives comes not from money but from the love of others. As you grow your business, please do not forget that spending time with your loved ones is job 1. No amount of money can serve as a substitute for the love of family and friends. Two of the five biggest regrets most people have before they die are "I wish I hadn't worked so hard" and "I wish I had stayed in touch with my friends."[143]

I know I am preaching to the choir.

But I just wanted to make sure.

In recent years I have met a number of young entrepreneurs who have accumulated a half dozen or so properties, and one thing they seem to have in common is a frenetic personality. They worry a lot about their

---

[143]The five biggest regrets are (1) "I wish I'd had the courage to live a life true to myself, not the life others expected of me," (2) "I wish I hadn't worked so hard," (3) "I wish I'd had the courage to express my feelings," (4) "I wish I had stayed in touch with my friends," and (5) "I wish I had let myself be happier." Beverlee Warren, "The Top Five Regrets of the Dying: A Life Transformed by the Dearly Departing by Bronnie Ware," Proceedings (Baylor University Medical Center), 25(3): 299–300 (July 2012), retrieved 1/17/23 from <https://www.ncbi.nlm.nih.gov/pmc/articles/PMC3377309>.

properties and they are consumed with finding the next deal.

Don't become one of those entrepreneurs. Keep your life balanced.

Okay, let's turn to the main issue of this chapter: How to grow your rental business.

Three Ways to Buy Another Rental

Your first property is doing so well that you now have enough income to afford to purchase another rental.

Wonderful.

But most new real estate investors aren't this lucky. Even with a successful rental, they still don't have enough income to qualify for a conventional loan for a new rental nor enough cash for a down payment.

There are at least three options to overcome this problem.

- *Find Other Investors.* I covered this option in Chapters 8 and 9.

- *Obtain a Debt-Service Coverage Ratio Loan.* As I noted in Chapter 2, that's what I did, because I didn't have enough income to qualify for a conventional loan.

- *Do a 1031 Exchange.* This involves selling your property and investing in a more expensive property. One of the advantages of this is that your depreciation recapture tax is wiped out and your capital gains taxes are deferred.

Debt-Service Coverage Ratio Loan

A conventional loan is based on your earned income.

In other words, do you have enough income to cover the mortgage payment?

In contrast, a DSCR loan is based on your rental business's cash flow.[144] Is it high enough to cover your real estate expenses and the new mortgage?

The formula for calculating the ratio is simple:

$$\text{NET OPERATING INCOME} \div \text{DEBT SERVICE}$$

So if your rental business is generating $40,000 a year in income and your expenses are $20,000, your ratio is 2. You have enough income to cover all of your expenses plus $20,000 more. If your debt service is $40,000, you have a ratio of 1, which means you are meeting all expenses but do not have any profits. Most lenders use a ratio of 1.2 to 1.25 as a minium for a loan. A ratio of 2 is very good.

Net operating income includes revenues but not taxes and interest payments on loans. Debt service refers to all debt obligations, including interest, principal, and lease payments. Calculating the ratio can be more complicated than this, because interest payments are tax deductible. Each lending institution also will have its own criteria to use in deciding whether to approve your loan. Some will require collateral. Your credit rating will also be a factor.

When I applied for the DSCR loan in 2022, I had no outstanding debt. I owned my house outright, which, at that time, was valued at $460,000. The income from my rental home was about $3,600 a month. My costs were about $905 a month (I had no mortgage payments). So my ratio was nearly 4, which is really high. I also had a good credit

---

[144]There are a lot of resources on the web with respect to DSCR loans. Here are two: Jason Fernando, "Debt-Service Coverage Ratio (DSCR): How to Use and Calculate It," Investopedia (Dec. 04, 2023), retrieved 1/17/24 from <https://www.investopedia.com/terms/d/dscr.asp> and "What Is A DSCR Loan? And How Do They Work?" We Lend LLC (April 27, 2023), retrieved 1/17/24 from <https://www.welendllc.com/blog/what-is-a-dscr-loan>.

rating and the lender required me to use my property as collateral for the loan. Not all DSCR loans require collateral but, as you might expect, the interest rates will be higher if collateral is not offered.

DSCR loans are attractive to real estate investors because they provide a way to finance investments without putting a large amount of money down. The DSCR requirement ensures that the property generates enough income to cover the loan payments, which reduces the risk for the lender and makes it more likely that the loan will be approved. Additionally, since the loan is based on the property's income, the investor's personal income and creditworthiness are less important factors in the loan approval process.

A DSCR loan is attractive because a borrower doesn't have to put down a down payment to buy the next property. The loan covers almost everything except closing costs.

Doing a 1031 Exchange

If you don't have enough money to buy another rental property or the 1.2+ ratio to qualify for a DSCR loan, you could build your portfolio and income with a 1031 exchange. This involves selling your property and buying another one of greater value and potentially greater rental revenues.

You could, for example, sell you rental home or condo and buy a duplex, which could produce twice the revenues without twice the expense. Another advantage of a 1031 is that you don't have to pay the depreciation recapture tax on your previous property, which could save you a bundle depending on how many years you depreciated the property. The capital gains taxes on the property you sold are also deferred until you sell the new, more expensive property.

A *1031 Exchange* (also known as a "Starker Exchange," under Section 1031 of the IRS Code) allows an investor to defer paying capital gains taxes as long as another "like-kind property" is purchased with the profit gained by the sale of the first property.

You can basically exchange a single-family rental property for another property like it, or a condo, duplex, commercial office building or apartment community. The only requirement is that the purchase price and new loan must be the same or higher than for your original property.

When you sell the first property, your proceeds are held by a third party who uses it to purchase the replacement property for you. Most investors need experts to ensure they comply fully with the law. There are four types of exchanges:

- *Delayed.* This exchange is the most common type and occurs when the *exchangor* sells the original property before acquiring the replacement property. The exchangor has 45 days to identify the replacement property and 180 days to buy the replacement.

- *Simultaneous.* This exchange involves selling and buying the properties on the same day. Any delay can cancel the exchange and full taxes can be assessed.

- *Reverse.* Also known as a *forward exchange*, this involves buying a replacement property and paying for it later. The reverse exchange is done in cash. The exchangor must decide which of her or his investment properties will be relinquished. Failing to close in 180 days will result in a forfeit of the exchange. The exchangor has 45 days to identify the property to be relinquished and must complete the sale of the replacement property within 135 days.

- *Construction.* This exchange allows the exchangor to use her tax-deferred dollars to enhance or remodel the replacement property while it's under the control of an intermediary for the remainder of the 180-day period. The replacement property must be of equal or greater value when deeded to the exchangor. The improvements must be complete before obtaining the deed.

One of the big advantages of a 1031 exchange is that the depreciation recapture tax on the property you sell is eliminated. Depreciation starts anew on the replacement property and you will have to pay a recapture tax when you sell it, but you'll be paying less overall. In fact, if you owned the original property for many years, your tax savings could be in the thousands of dollars. And if you sell the replacement property after a year or two, the recapture tax will be relatively small.

However, if you purchased the replacement property with the express purpose of avoiding recapture taxes on the original property, you might be required to pay recapture taxes. The law assumes you bought the replacement property for investment purposes, not to avoid paying taxes.[145]

---

[145]See opinion from Asset Preservation Incorporated, retrieved January 26, 2024, from <https://apiexchange.com/how-long-to-hold>.

How to Increase Rates and Cut Costs

If you can't buy another property to boost your profits, you can step up your profits by increasing your rental rates, by cutting costs, and by living in your rental unit to save on capital gains expenses.

Raising Your Rental Rates

Rental rates in the United States soared from 2020 to 2023.

Single-family home rental rates grew 36 percent, from $1,560 to $2,122, and multifamily units grew 23 percent, from $1,485 to $1,826.[146] The increases outpaced the increases in income, making it more difficult for working Americans to find affordable housing.

Here are some of the factors that have been cited to explain these increases, according to Nerdwallet:

- *Inflation.* Inflation increased nearly 18 percent from 2020 to 2023.[147] Landlords are passing higher costs (including rising wages for maintenance workers, landlord insurance, and repair costs) to renters.

---

[146]Ann Helhoski, "Rental Market Trends in the U.S. — Rental Price Growth Cooled in December," Nerdwallet (Jan. 11, 2024), retrieved 1/17/24 from <https://nerdwallet.com/article/finance/rental-market-trends>.

[147]This estimate was obtained from an inflation calculator posted (retrieved 1/17/24) at <https://www.usinflationcalculator.com>.

Higher rents, in turn, contribute to inflation, fueling the cycle even more. Many economic analyses also conclude that half of the inflation rate is fueled by the band wagon effect ("everyone else is raising prices, so we should, too") and greed.[148]

- *Lack of inventory.* There is a shortage of vacant rental properties, especially affordable ones. Estimates range from 1.5 million to 3.8 million.[149] This has been the case in the United States for many years.

- *Expired rent freezes/discounts.* The federal government forced landlords to stop evicting people who could not pay their rent during the pandemic years (2020–2022). Landlords are now hiking prices to make up losses.

- *A shifting workforce.* Deep-pocketed renters who worked from home sought larger homes in areas that had been previously relatively low-cost. This migration allegedly boosted rents in suburban areas.

- *More demand to live alone.* Demand for studio and one-bedroom apartments has increased. One factor is that nearly a third of Americans live alone. In 1940, only 8 percent lived alone.[150]

- *Barriers to home ownership.* High interest rates and home prices have kept prospective homeowners at bay. Supply chain disruptions also made it more expensive and difficult to construct new homes.

---

[148]Julia Mueller, "'Greedflation' Is the New Inflation as Corporate Profits Balloon," *The Hill* (June 6, 2023), retrieved 1/17/24 from <https://thehill.com/business/economy/4057722-greedflation-is-the-new-inflation-as-corporate-profits-balloon-report>.

[149]"The State of Housing 2023: More Multifamily Housing, But the Shortage Persists," California Yimby Blog (August 10, 2023), retrieved 1/17/24 from <https://cayimby.org/blog/the-state-of-housing-2023-more-multifamily-housing-but-the-shortage-persists>.

[150]Janae Bowens, "Rising Trend of Living Solo: New Census Data Reveals Nearly 30% of American Households Are Single Occupancy," CBS Austin (July 10, 2023), retrieved 1/17/24 from <https://cbsaustin.com/news/nation-world/new-data-shows-nearly-1-out-of-3-americans-is-living-alone-census-real-estate-single-at-heart-labor-force-market-social-isolation-loneliness-medicine-health-wellness-high-blood-pressure-anxiety>.

If you owned a rental during those times, you probably raised your rates. And if you didn't, you no doubt will have to in the future, especially if inflation continues to rise.

A Brief History of Rental Rates

Rental rates have risen faster than the rate of inflation.

In 1940, the average property was renting for $27 a month, compared to $2,000 today. That's an annualize rate increase of 5.3 percent, compared with about 3.7 percent for inflation. Since 2012, rents have increased at an average of 6.5 percent per year, more than twice as much as the inflation rate of 2.8 percent.[151]

The U.S. government recommends that renters spend about 30 percent or less of their income on rent. Most, though, are spending nearly 40 percent. Rental rates are sensitive to inflationary costs, but they also increase when mortgage rates increase. As the cost of buying a house increases, more people are forced to continue renting, which drives up demand and reduces the supply of rental property available.

The Costs and Benefits of Raising Rent

Your ability as a landlord to raise rental rates will depend partly on the history of rates in your market. Growing metropolitan areas tend to experience the fastest increases in rental rates. Rural areas and poor inner city areas experience the lowest increases.

Some real estate experts say you shouldn't raise rents by more than 5 percent on residents living in your units. With higher increases, some

---

[151]Rent statistics were obtained from Statista, retrieved October 3, 2024, from <https://www.statista.com/statistics/200223/median-apartment-rent-in-the-us-since-1980>, and inflation statistics were obtained from Official Data Foundation, <http://www.in2013dollars.com/1980-dollars-in-2017?amount=100>.

tenants will leave to find less expensive accommodations.[152] Your costs can also increase when residents leave, because you'll need to clean and fix up the rental, advertise to attract another tenant, and absorb the costs of a vacant unit, possibly for a month or more.

To illustrate, let's say you're renting your property for $1,200 a month. If you raise the rent 6 percent, you'll now get $72 more a month ($1,200 × .06) or $864 a year. However, if your tenant leaves, then you likely will lose a month of rent ($1,200), in addition to your costs of cleaning and repairing the unit ($250), and advertising to get a new tenant ($100). So you'll lose about $1,550. It will take you nearly two years to make up those losses ($72 × 23 months = $1,584).

If you have to raise rent, set the increase slightly below the inflation rate, which is usually about 3 to 4 percent. So set it at 2.9 percent. If you never increase your rental rate, in 10 years your rental income will drop by more than a third because inflation cheapens dollars over time. If you raise your rates by just 2 percent a year, at the end of 10 years you'll have 65 percent more revenue. That still won't keep up with inflation, but it will help your bottom line.

Ways to Reduce Costs

Reducing costs is a constant concern facing landlords, irrespective of whether they can raise rent rates to keep up with inflation. Here are some suggestions.

1. *Refinance Your Mortgage or Equity Loan.* Is the interest rate on your mortgage or equity loan too high? Refinancing is a way to substantially

---

[152]Sterling White, "Top 10 Reasons Tenants Move Out (And How to Keep Them)," BiggerPockets (March 1, 2021), retrieved January 26, 2024, from <www.biggerpockets.com/blog/reasons-tenants-leave>.

reduce your costs, assuming that interest rates have come down.

If you have equity in your rental, you could also take out some cash to use as a down payment on another property to pay off other debts. But be aware that you'll have closing costs that could run into the thousands of dollars. Refinance only if you intend to keep the property for a while.

2. *Look for New Independent Contractors.* In recent years, landscapers, electricians, plumbers, painters, tilers, and other professional contractors have increased their rates substantially, sometimes by more than 30 percent. Bid out your next job to see if you can find someone less expensive or do the work yourself.

3. *Change Insurance Companies.* In recent years, many insurance companies have increased their rates, often outpacing inflation. Check first to make sure you aren't over insured. If your rental is worth $300,000 but you have $500,000 in coverage, you are paying extra and, if there is a loss claim, your company will not pay you the full $500,000. Most policies stipulate replacement costs only.

If over-insuring isn't a problem, get some bids to see if you can beat your current rate. To reduce your workload, hire an independent insurance agent, who can search many companies to find you the best rate.

4. *Appeal Your Taxes.* Are you paying too much in property taxes? This doesn't happen a lot. Most tax records undervalue properties. Appraisers do this to reduce appeals, which are costly and time-consuming to adjudicate.

There is a bias in the appraisal business. But it favors more expensive properties and businesses than lower priced homes and properties. A computerized scientific analysis several decades ago found that owners of higher-priced properties were paying less than their fair share in taxes.[153]

So, if your property is lower priced, there is a greater chance that it is over-assessed. One way to confirm this is to check the tax rates on values of properties near yours at Zillow. Note, though, that in some jurisdictions, state laws limit how much property taxes can be increased. So the records (and the size of the tax bills) are not updated until the property is sold.

If you think the government is charging you too much in taxes, you can file an appeal. The only downside is that this can take up your time. If you can't save several thousand dollars, it might not be worth it.

5. *Try Advertising through Signage.* Online or newspaper advertising to attract tenants can be expensive if you just have one property. Instead, try putting up a "For Rent" sign on your lawn, which is much cheaper. This works best when you have a fair amount of traffic that passes by your property. If your property is in a cul-de-sac, however, it may be difficult for people to see your sign.

6. *Insulate Your Attic.* If you have to pay the gas and electric bills on your rental and they are high, you might consider adding insulation in the attic. That can reduce your bills. However, you should do an informal cost/benefit analysis, because it could take many years to recover the costs of installing the insulation.

7. *Switch to Streaming Services.* If you are operating a short-term rental, you'll have to provide some kind of television programming service for your guests. Cable can be expensive. On my property, I offer local broadcast channels, Netflix, and Amazon Prime. I pay about $30 a month, versus $60+ for satellite TV and $100+ for cable. I have never

---

[153]Mark Engebretson and David Pearce Demers, "Assessing Damage: Unfair Property Tax Assessments Cause Working-class Homeowners and Renters to Pay Too Much, While Owners of Businesses, Farms, and Expensive Homes Don't Pay Enough," *Twin Cities Reader* (March 20–26, 1991), pp. 10–13.

received a complaint from a guest. Of course, you also have to offer internet service free of charge.

8. *Do Your Own Taxes.* As you have already read in this book, I am a big fan of doing your own taxes. The software programs are less than $100 and make it easy. An accountant or tax expert will charge much more than that. However, when you have a complex problem or issue, consult those experts or a tax attorney.

How to Reduce Your Capital Gains Tax

Previously I talked about how you can reduce your depreciation recapture taxes (see Chapter 21). I also talked about how you can defer your capital gains taxes by doing a 1031 exchange. This does not eliminate the capital gains taxes. It only defers them.

Now I want to show you how to reduce your capital gains taxes.

When you sell your rental property, you will have to pay capital gains taxes on the difference between what you paid for the property and the selling price (minus capital improvements).

If you are single and your income is between $44,625 and $492,301, your capital gains tax rate will be 15 percent ($89,251 to $553,850 for married couples). So, if you made a profit of $100,000, you pay about $15,000 in taxes. (The top capital gains tax rate is 20 percent.)

(*Did I hear someone say OUCH?*) There are three major ways to reduce or eliminate your capital gains taxes.

Live on Your Property

You can reduce or eliminate capital gains taxes if you (1a) own the property for at least two of the previous five years before selling it or (1b) use the home as your primary residence for at least two of the past five years, and (2) if you have no excluded capital gains tax from any other sale in the last two years.

If you meet these criteria, tax law allows you to exclude up to $500,000 in taxable capital gains for married couples or $250,000 for single taxpayers. For example, let's say you purchase a property for $300,000 and after a year sell it for $400,000. The capital gains tax due would be $15,000 for middle-income earners. If you lived in the home for at least two of the previous five years or moved back in and lived in it for the last two years, your capital gains tax would be zero.

Consult a tax professional to make sure you qualify.

Harvest Your Tax Losses

If you own two or more properties and you sell one at a loss and the other at a gain in the same year, you can reduce your overall taxable capital gains and offset some of your taxable income.

For example, if you have a $100,000 gain from the sale of one rental and a $50,000 loss on the sale of another, your capital gain would be $50,000 instead of $100,000. So timing is everything. Pay attention to the losses and gains on your properties to minimize your tax bill.

Bequeath Your Property

If you own a rental property and you die, your heirs will not be required to pay capital gains on the property when they sell it. It's wise to have a trust or will that spells out who will inherit your property. In some areas, you can also use a beneficiary deed, which is easy to draft. The property averts probate court and goes directly to your heirs.

Appendices

APPENDIX 1

2023 Profit Estimates for My Short-Term Rental Home vs. Stock Market

— $35,000 Down on a $285,000 DSCR Loan with a 9.25% 30-Year Fixed Interest Loan —

	ESTIMATED PROFITS		ESTIMATED INCOME FROM RENTAL			DEPRECIATION		ESTIMATED EXPENSES FROM RENTAL PROPERTY				
	A	B	C	D	E	F		G	H	I	J	K
Year	Stocks Gain – 7.5% per year since 1970, compounded — $35,000 Invested/ Yearly Profit	Rental Property Gain (C+D+E+Fa) – (G+H+I+J+K) — $35,000 Invested/ Yearly Profit	Equity from Appreciation (5% per year compounded) — Home Valued at $460,000 when leased	Rental Income ($4,600 per month x 12 = $55,200) — 4% rent increase per year compound	Equity from Principal Payments — Increases as interest payment decreases	House $159,000 Pool $40,200 New roof $4,950 Treated as an expense but no out-of-pocket cost/ Reduces taxes — Tax Savings	Total Deduction	Mortgage Payments — 30-Year $285,000 fixed loan at 9.25%	Landlord Insurance — 8% increase per year compound	Property Taxes — 6% increase per year compound	Maintenance/ Repair/ Landscaping/ Reserve fund — 5% increase per year compounded	Utilities– Electricity, Water, TV, Gas, Internet, Trash etc. — 5% increase per year compounded
1	$2,625	$42,387	$23,000	$55,200	$1,850	$1,338	$6,267	$28,136	$1,300	$1,763	$2,300	$5,502
2	$2,822	$45,324	$24,150	$57,408	$2,029	$1,338	$6,267	$28,136	$1,404	$1,869	$2,415	$5,777
3	$3,034	$48,390	$25,358	$59,704	$2,225	$1,338	$6,267	$28,136	$1,516	$1,981	$2,536	$6,066
4	$3,261	$51,588	$26,625	$62,092	$2,439	$1,338	$6,267	$28,136	$1,638	$2,100	$2,663	$6,369
5	$3,506	$54,931	$27,957	$64,576	$2,675	$1,338	$6,267	$28,136	$1,769	$2,226	$2,796	$6,688
6	$3,769	$58,422	$29,354	$67,159	$2,933	$1,338	$6,267	$28,136	$1,910	$2,359	$2,935	$7,022
7	$4,051	$62,067	$30,822	$69,846	$3,216	$1,338	$6,267	$28,136	$2,063	$2,501	$3,082	$7,373
8	$4,355	$65,873	$32,363	$72,639	$3,526	$1,338	$6,267	$28,136	$2,228	$2,651	$3,236	$7,742
9	$4,682	$69,852	$33,981	$75,545	$3,867	$1,338	$6,267	$28,136	$2,406	$2,810	$3,398	$8,129
10	$5,033	$74,009	$35,681	$78,567	$4,240	$1,338	$6,267	$28,136	$2,599	$2,979	$3,568	$8,535
Total Gain	$37,138	$572,843	$289,291	$662,736	$29,000	$13,380	$62,670	$281,360	$18,833	$23,239	$28,929	$69,203
ROI	$37,138 / $35,000 = 106%	$572,843 / $35,000 = 1,637%										

Total Estimated Income First 10 Years (Includes Tax Savings from Depreciation) $994,407

Total Estimated Expenses First 10 Years (Excluding Depreciation) $421,564

NOTES TO APPENDIX 1

Dollar amounts calculated at the end of each year. Starting year is 2023. Not adjusted for inflation.

A= Industry estimates of stock gains vary, depending upon dates and indices. For this analysis, I used the S&P 500, which is more robust than the using data for the entire market, which produces lower gains. From 1970 to 2022, the S&P 500 grew from 92 to 3,850 (see Macrotrends <https://www.macrotrends.net/2324/sp-500-historical-chart-data>), which is a 7,208 percent increase and an average annual gain of 7.5% (compounded). The $2,625 stock market profit in year 1 is derived by multiplying $35,000 by 7.5%. The figures for subsequent years are compounded.

B= These figures are derived by subtracting estimated expenses from estimated income.

C= An appraisal when I obtained the $285,000 loan put the value of my home at $460,000. Census Bureau and HUD data from 1970 to 2022 show that home values increased an average of 5.9% per year — from about $23,900 to $480,000 (Source: U.S. Census Bureau and U.S. Department of Housing and Urban Development, "Median Sales Price of Houses Sold for the United States" [MSPUS], retrieved from FRED, Federal Reserve Bank of St. Louis, retrieved June 8, 2023, from <https://fred.stlouisfed.org/series/MSPUS>). I used a 5% appreciation rate to create more conservative future estimates.

D= My average rental income during 2022 was $3,600 per month and during 2023 was $4,600. The latter equates to an annual gross income of $55,200. The average annual increase in monthly rent in the United States is 5.6% a year (see June Blog, "How U.S. Rent Prices Have Changed Over Time," retrieved from <https://junehomes.com/blog/2022/09/09/how-rent-prices-the-have-changed-over-time>). However, to estimate future income, I used a conservative estimate of 4%.

E= The equity (principal) payments on the mortgage are based on an interest rate of 9.25% on a $285,000 loan.

F= The depreciation deduction is based on the cost of the property minus the value of the land, which is usually estimated at 20% of the total purchase price. Since I paid $159,000 for the property, that meant $127,200 was eligible for depreciation. The IRS allows a home to be depreciated over 27.5 years, which means a deduction of $4,625 per year (the first year deduction is slightly less, but I did not include it here because it complicates things more than needed for this illustration). In addition to depreciating the house, I depreciated two other improvements to the property — a $40,200 swimming pool I installed and a $4,950 new roof, which brought the total deduction to $6,267. I used TurboTax Home & Business 2022 to generate the depreciation figures.

G= The mortgage payments are based on a $285,000 DSCR loan. A DSCR loan is based on the income of the property, not the borrower's income. I had six months of rental receipts when I obtained the loan in December 2022. I used the loan to purchase a $250,000 two-bedroom, two-bathroom condominium, in which I now live and lease half of it to a relative. The remainder of the loan was used for closing costs and other business expenses. The total mortgage payments each year come to $28,136, which includes interest and principal payments.

H= My landlord insurance policy through Traveler's cost $1,300 a year in 2023 ($300,000 liability; replacement costs). I could not locate statistics on price increases for landlord insurance over time, but homeowners insurance increased about 59% from 2010 to 2020, going from $909 to $1,445 (PR Newswire, "Homeowners Insurance Premiums Increased 59% Over The Past Decade," June 4, 2020, retrieved from <https://www.prnewswire.com/news-releases/homeowners-insurance-premiums-increased-59-over-the-past-decade-valuepenguincom-finds-301070517.html>). That translates into a yearly increase of about 5%. Insurance rates increase not only because of inflation but also when the stock market loses value or remains stagnant. When the market drops and insurance investments lose value, insurance companies increase insurance rates to compensate for the losses (Source: FastrackCE, "How Does the Stock Market Affect Insurance Rates?" April 28, 2012, retrieved from <https://www.fastrackce.com/continuing-education/insurance/how-does-the-stock-market-affect-insurance-rates>). Many people object to this practice because they don't think it's right to punish consumers for investment mistakes. But that's the way the system works. I decided to go conservative and build in an 8% increase in insurance costs per year.

I= The property taxes on my home rental were $1,763 in 2022 (paid in 2023). In Arizona, increases in tax rates are limited to no more than 5% a year under a 2012 law. I set the increase at 6% to err on the conservative side.

J= For the maintenance and repair budget, I used the square-footage formula (1% of the square footage of a home) and then added $400 more in supplies for the swimming pool ($1,900 + $400 = $2,300). I assumed costs would rise about 5% per year thereafter.

K= My electric utility bill is about $314 per month and $3,762 annually. The remaining $1,740 pays for the water/sewer/trash/recycling ($60 per month), internet ($60 per month), and Amazon TV and Netflix ($25 a month). I assumed costs would rise about 5% per year thereafter.

APPENDIX 2

Profit Estimates for a $300,000 Rental Home vs. Stock Market

— Down Payment of $75,000 on a 30-Year Fixed 7% Interest Mortgage Loan —

	ESTIMATED PROFITS			ESTIMATED INCOME FROM RENTAL PROPERTY				DEPRECIATION		ESTIMATED EXPENSES FROM RENTAL PROPERTY				
	A	B		C	D		E	F		G	H	I	J	
Year	Stocks Gain – 7.5% Per Year Since 1970, compounded	Long- and Short-Term Rental Property Gain $75,000 Invested (C+D+E+Fa) – (G+H+I+J)		Equity from Appreciation 5% per year compound	Annual Rental Income 4% rent increase per year compounded		Equity from Principal Payments	$300,000 House/ 1/27.5 of $240,000 (excludes land)/ Treated as an expense but no out-of-pocket cost/ Can reduce taxes Tax Savings Total Long/Short Deduction		Mortgage Payment	Property Taxes and Landlord Insurance	Maintenance/ Repair/ Reserve	–Utilities– Water/Sewer/Trash for long-term rental/ Electric/gas/internet TV-cable for short	
	$75,000 Invested Yearly Profit	Long-term Invested/ Yearly Profit	Short-term Invested/ Yearly Profit	Based on $300,000 purchase price	Long-term rental/ $2,200 per month	Short-term/ $4,400 per month	Increases as interest decreases			30-Year $225,000 Loan at 7% Fixed	6% increase per year compound	5% increase per year compound	5% Long-term rental	6% Short-term rental
1	$5,625	$17,775	$41,049	$15,000	$26,400	$52,800	$2,286	$8,727	$0/$726	$17,963	$4,400	$2,600	$948	$4,800
2	$6,047	$19,295	$43,442	$15,750	$27,456	$54,912	$2,451	$8,727	$0/$726	$17,963	$4,664	$2,730	$1,005	$5,040
3	$6,500	$20,881	$45,934	$16,538	$28,554	$57,108	$2,628	$8,727	$0/$726	$17,963	$4,944	$2,867	$1,065	$5,292
4	$6,988	$22,536	$48,531	$17,364	$29,696	$59,393	$2,818	$8,727	$0/$726	$17,963	$5,240	$3,010	$1,129	$5,557
5	$7,512	$24,264	$51,238	$18,233	$30,884	$61,769	$3,022	$8,727	$0/$726	$17,963	$5,555	$3,160	$1,197	$5,834
6	$8,075	$26,066	$54,054	$19,144	$32,120	$64,239	$3,240	$8,727	$0/$726	$17,963	$5,888	$3,318	$1,269	$6,126
7	$8,681	$27,945	$56,989	$20,101	$33,404	$66,809	$3,474	$8,727	$0/$726	$17,963	$6,242	$3,484	$1,345	$6,432
8	$9,332	$29,911	$60,048	$21,107	$34,741	$69,481	$3,725	$8,727	$0/$726	$17,963	$6,616	$3,658	$1,425	$6,754
9	$10,032	$31,959	$63,234	$22,162	$36,130	$72,260	$3,995	$8,727	$0/$726	$17,963	$7,013	$3,841	$1,511	$7,092
10	$10,784	$34,097	$66,555	$23,270	$37,575	$75,151	$4,284	$8,727	$0/$726	$17,963	$7,434	$4,033	$1,602	$7,446
Total Gain	$79,576	$254,729	$531,074	$188,669	$316,960	$633,922	$31,923	$87,270	$0/$7,260	$179,630	$57,996	$32,701	$12,496	$60,373
ROI	$79,576 / $75,000 = 106%	$254,729 / $75,000 = 340%	$531,074 / $75,000 = 708%											

ESTIMATED INCOME FROM RENTAL PROPERTY
Total Estimated Income First 10 Years (Includes Tax Savings from Depreciation)
Long-term Rental $537,552   Short-term Rental $861,774

ESTIMATED EXPENSES FROM RENTAL PROPERTY
Total Estimated Expenses First 10 Years
Long-term Rental $282,823   Short-term Rental $330,700

NOTES TO APPENDIX 2

Dollar amounts calculated at the end of each year. Starting year is 2023. Not adjusted for inflation.

A= Over the past 52 years (1970 to 2022), the value of S&P stocks has grown from 92 to 3,840, an average annual gain of 7.5% (compounded, see Macrotrends at https://www.macrotrends.net/2324/sp-500-historical-chart-data). The $5,625 profit in year 1 is derived from multiplying $75,000 by 7.5%. The amounts for subsequent years are compounded.

B= Annual profits from a $300,000 rental home are derived by subtracting estimated expenses from estimated income. Results from long-term and short-term renting are shown. The amounts for long-term are smaller because it generates less rental income and does not benefit from depreciation because the total income is too small. A tax deduction will show up, however, if the investor received earned income from another job.

C= Equity from appreciation is based on a home valuation of $300,000. Census Bureau and HUD data from 1970 to 2022 show that home values increased an average of 5.9% per year — from about $23,900 to $480,000 (Source: U.S. Census Bureau and U.S. Department of Housing and Urban Development, "Median Sales Price of Houses Sold for the United States" [MSPUS], retrieved from FRED, Federal Reserve Bank of St. Louis, retrieved June 8, 2023, from <https://fred.stlouisfed.org/series/MSPUS>). I used a 5% appreciation rate to create more conservative estimates.

D= In 2023, the median rental rate in the United States was nearly $2,000 a month, according to Rent.com (https://www.rent.com/research/average-rent-price-report/). This figure includes both apartments and homes. I set the price of a rental home at $2,200 a month, because homes have nearly twice as much square footage as apartments, 2,000 vs. 900 (see The Ascent, <www.fool.com/the-ascent/mortgages/articles/how-big-is-your-home-here-is-the-average-home-size-by-state> and RentCafe, <https://www.rentcafe.com/average-rent-market-trends/us>). Many real estate experts say that a short-term rental draws three to five times as much income as a long-term rental, but my experience doesn't support this. So I went conservative and set the short-term rental income at $4,400 a month, which is slightly lower than the income generated on my property (see Appendix 1) and less than twice as much as a long-term lease. The average annual increase in monthly rent in the United States is 5.6% a year (see June Blog, "How U.S. Rent Prices Have Changed Over Time," retrieved from <https://junehomes.com/blog/2022/09/09/how-rent-prices-the-have-changed-over-time>), but I used a conservative estimate of 4% to calculate future rental income.

E= Principal payments on a $225,000 mortgage are estimated using a fixed interest rate of 7%. The amounts were derived using an online calculator at <https://www.calculatestuff.com/financial/mortgage-calculator>. Note that the mortgage payment (see column G) also includes the principal, but it comes back as income because it contributes to equity in the property. The first year principal payments are $2,286. The amount increases as the interest rate payment declines.

F= The depreciation deduction is based on the cost of the property minus the value of the land, which is usually estimated at 20% of the total purchase price if your state does not include it in the assessed valuation. In this case, it means that $240,000 was eligible for depreciation ($60,000 is the value of the land). The IRS allows a home to be depreciated over 27.5 years, which means a deduction of $8,727 per year (the first year deduction is slightly less, but I did not include it here because it complicates the analysis more than needed for this illustration).

G= The mortgage payments (interest and principal) are based on a $225,000 loan. The first-year interest deduction is $15,678, and this figure declines slightly every year until the 10th year, when the interest payment is $13,680. To calculate the actual tax savings, I used the 2022 Home and Business TurboTax program and estimated rental incomes of $52,800 (short-term) and $26,400 (long-term). If you already own a home that is mortgaged, you don't need to do anything more except put your property up for rent and find a place to live. If you already own a rental property and don't have enough income to qualify for another loan, you can use the income from your rental to obtain a DSCR loan. See text for more details.

Assuming an annual gross income of $52,800 on the property, the depreciation deduction reduces the tax bill by about $726 a year for a short-term rental. There is no deduction for a long-term rental, because the income is not high enough to qualify for a deduction (the other deductions and expenses were greater than the income). In both cases, the federal tax bill at the end of the year is zero or close to it. But the benefit from depreciation does grow bigger if the landlord earns money from other sources. In other words, the tax savings are maximized with the higher income. If you have negative income from the rental, IRS rules do allow you to carry that amount into the next year or future years, when you can use it offset future income.

H= I set the landlord insurance policy cost at $1,400, which is slightly higher than the policy that I have on my $460,000 home ($1,300 through Traveler's; $300,000 liability; replacement costs). I could not find statistics on average price increases for landlord insurance over time, but homeowners insurance increased about 59% from 2010 to 2020, going from $909 to $1,445 (PR Newswire, "Homeowners Insurance Premiums Increased 59% Over The Past Decade," June 4, 2020, retrieved from <https://www.prnewswire.com/news-releases/homeowners-insurance-premiums-increased-59-over-the-past-decade-valuepenguincom-finds-301070517.html>). That translates into a yearly increase of about 5%. Insurance rates increase not only because of inflation but also when the stock market loses value or remains stagnant. Insurance companies typically increase insurance rates to compensate for the losses (see FastrackCE, "How Does the Stock Market Affect Insurance Rates?" (April 28, 2012), retrieved from <www.fastrackce.com/continuing-education/insurance/how-does-the-stock-market-affect-insurance-rates>). Many people criticize this practice, because consumers essentially are being punished for mistakes made by insurance companies. I decided to go conservative and build in a 6% increase (compounded) in insurance costs per year. I estimated property taxes at $3,000 a year, which is the national average for a $300,000 home, according to Motley Fool (https://www.fool.com/research/property-tax-rates-by-state). I set the annual rate increase at 6% as well.

I= For the maintenance and repair budget, I used the square-footage formula (1% of square footage per year) and then added $600 more. I assumed costs would rise about 5% per year thereafter.

J= Forbes estimates the average utility bill nationwide is $4,800 for a typical home, which includes electric, natural gas, water, sewer, trash, cable TV, internet, phone, and security (https://www.forbes.com/home-improvement/living/monthly-utility-costs-by-state). Long-term utility rates are lower because tenants usually pay for all utilities except water, sewer, and trash pickup. I assumed costs for short-term rentals would rise 6% per year (compounded) and costs would rise 5% for long-term rentals, because those costs are less elastic than the other utilities.

APPENDIX 3

Profit Estimates for a $300,000 FHA Funded Home vs. Stock Market

— Down Payment of $14,000 (3.5% of selling price) on a 30-Year Fixed 7% Interest Mortgage Loan —

	ESTIMATED PROFITS		ESTIMATED INCOME FROM RENTAL PROPERTY			DEPRECIATION		ESTIMATED EXPENSES FROM RENTAL PROPERTY			
	A	B	C	D	E	F	G	H	I	J	
Year	Stocks Gain – 7.5% Per Year Since 1970, compounded	Long- and Short-Term Rental Property Gain $14,000 Invested (C+D+E+Fa) – (G+H+I+J)	Equity from Appreciation 5% per year compound	Annual Rental Income 4% rent increase per year compounded	Equity from Principal Payments	DEPRECIATION $300,000 House/ 1/27.5 of $240,000 (excludes land)/ Treated as an expense but no out-of-pocket cost/ Can reduce taxes	Mortgage Payment	Property Taxes and Landlord Insurance	Maintenance/ Repair/ Reserve	—Utilities — Water/Sewer/Trash for long-term rental/ Electric/gas/internet TV-cable for short	
	$14,000 Invested/ Yearly Profit	Long-term Invested/ Yearly Profit / Short-term Invested/ Yearly Profit	Based on $300,000 purchase price	Long-term rental/ $2,200 per month / Short-term/ $4,400 per month	Increases as interest decreases	Tax Savings Long/Short — Total Deduction	30-Year $286,000 Loan at 7% Fixed	6% increase per year compound	5% increase per year compound	5% Long-term rental / 6% Short-term rental	
1	$1,050	$13,524 / $36,798	$15,000	$26,400 / $52,800	$2,905	$0/$726 / $8,727	$22,833	$4,400	$2,600	$948 / $4,800	
2	$1,129	$15,089 / $39,236	$15,750	$27,456 / $54,912	$3,115	$0/$726 / $8,727	$22,833	$4,664	$2,730	$1,005 / $5,040	
3	$1,213	$16,724 / $41,777	$16,538	$28,554 / $57,108	$3,341	$0/$726 / $8,727	$22,833	$4,944	$2,867	$1,065 / $5,292	
4	$1,304	$18,430 / $44,425	$17,364	$29,696 / $59,393	$3,582	$0/$726 / $8,727	$22,833	$5,240	$3,010	$1,129 / $5,557	
5	$1,402	$20,213 / $47,187	$18,233	$30,884 / $61,769	$3,841	$0/$726 / $8,727	$22,833	$5,555	$3,160	$1,197 / $5,834	
6	$1,507	$22,075 / $50,063	$19,144	$32,120 / $64,239	$4,119	$0/$726 / $8,727	$22,833	$5,888	$3,318	$1,269 / $6,126	
7	$1,620	$24,017 / $53,061	$20,101	$33,404 / $66,809	$4,416	$0/$726 / $8,727	$22,833	$6,242	$3,484	$1,345 / $6,432	
8	$1,742	$26,052 / $56,189	$21,107	$34,741 / $69,481	$4,736	$0/$726 / $8,727	$22,833	$6,616	$3,658	$1,425 / $6,754	
9	$1,823	$28,172 / $59,447	$22,162	$36,130 / $72,260	$5,078	$0/$726 / $8,727	$22,833	$7,013	$3,841	$1,511 / $7,092	
10	$2,013	$30,388 / $62,846	$23,270	$37,575 / $75,151	$5,445	$0/$726 / $8,727	$22,833	$7,434	$4,033	$1,602 / $7,446	
Total Gain	$14,803	$214,684 / $491,029	$188,669	$316,960 / $633,922	$40,578	$0/$7,260 / $87,270	$228,330	$57,996	$32,701	$12,496 / $60,373	
ROI	$14,803 / $14,000 / 106%	$214,684 / $14,000 / 1,533% — $491,029 / $14,000 / 3,507%									

Total Estimated Income First 10 Years (Includes Tax Savings from Depreciation)
Long-term Rental $546,207 Short-term Rental $870,429

Total Estimated Expenses First 10 Years
Long-term Rental = $331,523 Short-term Rental= $379,400
SEE NOTES FOR APPENDIX 2 FOR MORE INFORMATION ABOUT THIS TABLE.

Index

S

(*continued on next page*)

About the Author

Dr. David Demers worked as a newspaper reporter, market researcher, and professor of journalism and media sociology before retiring to spend more time writing books and managing his short-term rental properties.

He purchased his first property at age 65, when he was ghostwriting the best-selling *ABCs of Buying Rental Property* for Ken McElroy. Two years later Demers converted his home into a short-term rental.

Demers also has written nearly two dozen other scholarly, trade, and ghostwritten books. He earned a master's degree in sociology from The Ohio State University and a Ph.D. in mass communication from the University of Minnesota. He has earned numerous reporting, research, writing, and free speech awards.

He was the plaintiff in *Demers v. Austin*, a 2014 Ninth Circuit Court of Appeals landmark ruling which extended constitutional protection to faculty speech that criticizes administrators' policies and actions on issues of public concern related to teaching and scholarship.

He lives in Phoenix.